ACCLAIM FOR TODD WILBUR'S
TOP SECRET RECIPES SERIES

"There's something almost magically compelling about the idea of making such foods at home ... The allure is undeniable, and [the books are] stuffed with tidbits and lore you're unlikely to find anywhere else."
—*Boston Herald*

"The mission: Decode the secret recipes for America's favorite junk foods. Equipment: Standard kitchen appliances. Goal: Leak the results to a ravenous public."
—*USA Today*

"This is the cookbook to satisfy all your cravings."
—Juli Huss, author of *The Faux Gourmet*

TODD WILBUR is the author of *Top Secret Recipes*, *More Top Secret Recipes*, *Top Secret Restaurant Recipes*, *Top Secret Recipes Lite!*, *Low-Fat Top Secret Recipes*, and *Top Secret Recipes: Sodas, Smoothies, Spirits, & Shakes* (all available from Plume). When not taste-testing recipes on himself, his friends, or TV talk-show hosts, Todd lives in Las Vegas.

EVEN MORE
TOP
SECRET
RECIPES

More Amazing Kitchen Clones of America's Favorite Brand-Name Foods

TODD WILBUR

Illustrated by the Author

A PLUME BOOK

PLUME
Published by the Penguin Group
Penguin Putnam Inc., 375 Hudson Street, New York, New York 10014, U.S.A.
Penguin Books Ltd, 80 Strand, London WC2R 0RL England
Penguin Books Australia Ltd, Ringwood, Victoria, Australia
Penguin Books Canada Ltd, 10 Alcorn Avenue, Toronto, Ontario, Canada M4V 3B2
Penguin Books (N.Z.) Ltd, 182–190 Wairau Road, Auckland 10, New Zealand

Penguin Books Ltd, Registered Offices: Harmondsworth, Middlesex, England

First published by Plume, a member of Penguin Putnam Inc.

First Printing (Special Sales Edition), February 2002

10 9 8 7 6 5 4 3 2 1

To the best of the author's knowledge, the information regarding company backgrounds and product histories is true and accurate. Any misrepresentation of factual material is completely unintentional.

Ⓟ REGISTERED TRADEMARK—MARCA REGISTRADA

CIP data is available.
ISBN 0-452-28319-1

Printed in the United States of America
Set in Gill Sans Light

To Howard Stern and his radio show
for hanging out with me in the kitchen every morning.

CONTENTS

INTRODUCTION

When a popular, ex–NBA basketball player was recently in Las Vegas, he was having a wild night at the roulette table. Tens of thousands of dollars had changed hands and he was getting mighty hungry. Recognizing this, the pit boss insisted on setting up a complimentary spread of food for the athlete and his entourage. The casino was braced to serve anything and everything the wealthy players desired. A dining room was set up; waiters and chefs stood by anxiously awaiting the order. Would the fancy feast include piles of imported Russian beluga caviar? Broiled fresh Maine lobster? Roquefort-encrusted corn-fed filet mignon? What does a large hungry man and his large hungry friends order when money isn't an issue? To the casino's delight the request was a simple one: It required only one person to make a quick trip to a drive-thru window just off the strip. Within twenty minutes the private dining room featured a fabulous spread of hot, juicy Fatburgers with cheese, thick milkshakes, and french fries. The hungry gamblers were in hamburger hog heaven.

I know that feeling well. Although I've never been "comped" for more than the $5.99 buffet while gambling in Las Vegas, I do know what it's like to crave that special sinful something, when nothing else matters. You lock on hard to the thought of a particular favorite food—one of your edible guilty pleasures— knowing for certain that you just won't be as deeply satisfied by anything else. When craving a drippy Taco Bell Burrito Supreme, a plateful of Peking duck—as good as Peking duck is at the right moment—isn't going to do the job. Sure, when it's all over your stomach's full just the same, but the road you mowed getting there wasn't the most delicious route.

When it comes to winning over a persistent palate, second-string selections score a hollow victory. A cheesy hamburger, a gooey caramel-and-peanut-coated candy bar, a soft chocolate chip cookie flanked by a tall, cold glass of milk; these are life's simple pleasures, simply fulfilled. These drool-inducing delights call out to us in the middle of a tedious project at work, or in the sixth hour of a long holiday road trip, or while stranded on an island for six weeks with fifteen strangers and a bag full of rice. These are the foods that are notoriously ready when you are, when nothing else will do; they are dependably made and consistently good. These are the foods that this book is all about.

For ten years now I've been sharing my secret recipes for clone cuisine, both here in these *Top Secret Recipes* books and on the Web site at TopSecretRecipes.com. I've cloned recipes for drinks and for appetizers and entrees from well-known restaurant chains across the country, such as Chili's, T.G.I. Friday's, and Applebee's. I've even created lite clone recipes for favorite sweet-tooth munchables such as Cinnabon Cinnamon Rolls and Olive Garden Tiramisu. But the books that started it all, *Top Secret Recipes* and *More Top Secret Recipes*, are the books that this one follows up. Those books feature clone recipes for the delicious delicacies from fast food chains, and for candy bars, and cookies and snack cakes. I'm talking about clones for the Big Mac, Mrs. Fields Cookies, Snickers, Reese's Peanut Butter Cups, Twinkies, and Oreo Cookies. Some call it convenience food. Some call it junk food. It's the food that spontaneous cravings are made of. I call it all delicious.

Whatever you call it, these are the most popular brand-name foods in the world. And it's now time to journey back to the roots of *Top Secret Recipes* for even more clones of the famous convenience food we all hate to love and love to eat.

Even more than clones of drinks or duplicates of food from full-service restaurant chains, the stuff in this book amazes your diners when they know you made it in your kitchen. It's this food, that's manufactured by machines or finished by fast-food assembly lines, that can be the hardest for me to reproduce as home-made recipes. Yet, when the formula has finally been cracked, these products yield the most rewarding results. Perhaps it's the sense that these foods aren't supposed to be made at home that makes the experience so enjoyable—after all, these are the foods that manufacturers most often claim as "secret formulas."

You'll find a clone recipe in this book for KFC Extra Tasty Crispy Chicken, plus a recipe for re-creating McDonald's French Fries. And I've included a long-overdue technique for making your own version of Auntie Anne's Pretzels at home. You'll also learn how to make your own Baby Ruth candy bars, and Taco Bell tacos from the ground up. Heinz Ketchup has finally been tackled, along with clones for Boston Market Meatloaf, KFC Mashed Potatoes & Gravy, and even those Fatburgers enjoyed at the gambler's banquet in Las Vegas. This book holds more than 85 new clone recipes for all types of convenience food, presented with easy in-structions, simple ingredients, and a chunk or two of food lore. It's the biggest collection of convenience food recipes yet, and this cookbook should hold several favorites for everyone. Whether you're a beginning cook or a seasoned chef, be prepared to amaze your diners with these kitchen copies.

Much has changed in the food industry since the first *Top Se-cret Recipes* book came out in 1993. In the Introduction of that book I included a list of the top-grossing fast food chains in America based on 1991 sales. Now, ten years later, it's interesting to glance back at how much has changed in this volatile industry in just a decade (and then again, how much hasn't).

CHAIN	U.S. UNITS	'91 U.S. SALES (IN MILLIONS)
1. McDonald's	12,418	19,928.2
2. Burger King	6,409	6,200.0
3. KFC	8,480	6,200.0
4. Pizza Hut	9,000	5,300.0
5. Hardee's	3,727	3,431.0

CHAIN	U.S. UNITS	'91 U.S. SALES (IN MILLIONS)
6. Wendy's	3,804	3,223.6
7. Taco Bell	3,670	2,800.0
8. Domino's Pizza	5,500	2,400.0
9. Dairy Queen	5,329	2,352.4
10. Little Caesar	3,650	1,725.0
11. Arby's	2,500	1,450.0
12. Subway	6,106	1,400.0
13. Dunkin' Donuts	2,203	990.8
14. Jack in the Box	1,089	978.0
15. Baskin-Robbins	3,533	829.7
16. Carl's Jr.	630	614.0
17. Long John Silver's	1,450	555.0
18. Popeye's Chicken	808	540.2
19. Sonic Drive-Ins	1,112	518.0
20. Church's Chicken	1,136	506.6
21. Captain D's	636	420.8
22. Chick-fil-A	460	324.6
23. TCBY	1,850	321.0
24. Round Table Pizza	575	320.0
25. Whataburger	475	318.4

Source: *Nation's Restaurant News*

Since 1991, the planet's largest restaurant chain has focused almost all of its growth on McDonald's hamburger outlets overseas, with restaurants now located in 120 countries. Over 4000 of those stores are in Asia, including five of the world's busiest McDonald's. Even though the chain hasn't flexed its domestic hamburger muscle much, Ronald has been busy dotting the globe.

Along the way McDonald's scooped up the faltering Boston Market chain (a new addition to the top 25 fast food chains list in the last 10 years), with an initial plan to gut 1000 of the Boston Market units and crown them with the Golden Arches.

Mickey D's has diversified with other brands as well, including ownership in Donatos Pizza and Chipotle Mexican Grill. And don't be surprised if one day you're ordering a Grande McLatte at McDonald's new McCafe coffeehouse. This Starbucks-like coffee chain has already seen success in other countries, and will now be grinding the beans here on our shores with test units opening in select cities. Just when you thought you'd seen it all, if you're looking for a place to stay in Switzerland some day you may find rooms in one of two Golden Arch Hotels opened by

CHAIN	U.S. UNITS	'00 U.S. SALES (IN MILLIONS)
1. McDonald's	12,804	19,573.0
2. Burger King	8,064	8,695.0
3. Wendy's	5,095	5,813.4
4. Taco Bell	6,746	5,100.0
5. Pizza Hut	7,927	5,000.0
6. KFC	5,364	4,400.0
7. Subway	12,254	3,788.0
8. Domino's Pizza	4,818	2,647.2
9. Arby's	3,153	2,410.0
10. Dairy Queen	5,058	2,225.0
11. Dunkin' Donuts	3,641	2,178.0
12. Hardee's	2,526	2,027.6
13. Jack in the Box	1,634	1,921.3
14. Starbucks	2,700	1,785.0
15. Sonic Drive-Ins	2,175	1,778.8
16. Papa John's	2,533	1,669.0
17. Little Caesar's Pizza	3,290	1,110.0
18. Chick-fil-A	958	1,082.1
19. Popeye's Chicken	1,248	1,076.8
20. Carl's Jr.	945	1,002.8
21. Long John Silver's	1,195	761.6
22. Church's Chicken	1,217	698.7
23. Boston Market	712	685.0
24. Whataburger	550	559.0
25. Baskin-Robbins	2,435	554.0

Source: *Nation's Restaurant News*

the Swiss arm of McDonald's Corp. (French fries on the pillows at night?)

Ten years later Burger King still holds its position at second place with nearly 2000 units added since 1991. The King is closing the gap with McDonald's and has challenged the Golden Arches not only with the Big King (see clone recipe on page 26), a burger that looks and tastes similar to the Big Mac, but has altered its french fry formula twice in the last four years in the hopes of gaining some ground on the spud front. Unfortunately the Big King burger didn't catch on, and reviews for the first round of new fries came up soggy.

Wendy's moved up to number three from 1991, filling KFC's old slot. It seems burgers and sandwiches continue to thrive over fried chicken products. Hoping to ride the sandwich wave, KFC continues to develop new chicken sandwiches, despite some less than popular selections. Sure, the sandwiches are tasty, but not tasty enough to keep KFC's market share from shrinking. In the last decade the chain shuttered over 3000 domestic units, while converting many outlets into dual- or triple-brand multiconcept locations with parent company Tricon's other two brands, Taco Bell and Pizza Hut.

Taco Bell, however, nearly doubled its number of units since 1991 and moved up the ladder into fourth place. New products have bolstered the chain, as a talking Chihuahua coaxed us into munching on the occasional Gordita and Chalupa. The Bell has more recently been adding five-thousand-dollar grills to each restaurant to introduce a line of new grilled products that kicked off with the Grilled Stuft Burrito. Expect to see mucho other grilled offerings from the Bell in the future.

New product development was also important for Pizza Hut over the last decade. The Stuffed Crust Pizza, The Edge Pizza, and the Twisted Crust Pizza are several reasons why Pizza Hut remains the number-one pizza chain in the country, although competition from other chains (such as newcomer Papa John's) forced the Hut to close nearly 1000 units over the last decade, causing its overall fast food rank to fall from fourth to fifth place.

Subway was a big mover over the years, doubling its units

from 6000 to over 12,000. That number of units is up in McDonald's territory, but since total sales per store is low compared to McDonald's, Subway ranks down at seventh on the list. Still, that's up from twelfth a decade ago, helped in part by a promotional campaign with a weight loss angle. Perhaps you've seen the spots with Jared, the young man who melted the pounds away on a diet of Subway sandwiches. Okay, whatever. Personally, I'm still waiting for the diet of french fries and beer.

Arby's, Dairy Queen, and Jack in the Box maintained their same approximate positions in the list. But Hardee's, a struggling hamburger joint with units throughout the South, Midwest, and Eastern United States, slipped way down, from fifth to twelfth place with the closure of over 1000 stores.

Even though Dairy Queen stayed strong, losing only around 200 units, it looks like we don't do ice cream and frozen yogurt like we did ten years ago. Have creamy frozen confections been replaced by coffee drinks and donuts? TCBY is off the list and Baskin-Robbins dropped seven places, losing over 1000 units. Dunkin' Donuts continues to thrive, and farther down (just off the list at number 27) Krispy Kreme is quickly approaching with "hot donuts now" signs a-flashing.

Take note of the newcomers to the top 25, most impressive of which is the Papa John's pizza chain. In 1999, Papa John's breezed right past Little Caesar's. Now Papa John's is over 2500 units strong and is raking in almost two billion dollars in sales. That's impressive stuff from a guy who, 18 years ago, was baking pizzas out of an old oven in a converted broom closet. If you're a big Papa John's fan, I've got clones of John's sauces on page 165.

Starbucks is another new success story on the list. This huge coffee house chain started in 1987, and in only 13 years has grown to 2700 units—remarkable numbers when you consider that in 1991, there were only 116 of the now-famous coffee houses, and in the year 2000, Starbucks added more than 700 new stores! That's a lot of hot milk foam.

Boston Market, our third new addition to the list, reached its peak somewhere in the middle of the last decade right around the time it changed its name from Boston Chicken. Despite slipping from a total of over 1200 units to the current 700, the chain still hangs on to a position on the list at twenty-third place. Once on the move in a big way, Boston Market made its mark selling home-style chicken and side dishes. But in 1995, when the chain added other meat products to the menu such as turkey and meatloaf (check out the meatloaf clone recipe on page 22), the company changed its name. Once the sweetheart of the stock market, Boston Market's aggressive growth plus increased competition in what they call the "home meal replacement" category led to a 1998 bankruptcy. Ouch. Hungry McDonald's swooped in to score the company at a bargain price and quickly closed many of the underperforming units. The remaining 700 Boston Market stores are now a profitable business, and McDonald's has scrapped plans to convert them to more McDonald's.

It's not hard to see that the food industry is an extremely competitive one. That's bad news for restaurants, but good news for *Top Secret Recipes* fans. Stiff competition means a constant flow of new products for us to clone at home. In fact, as I write this, a jingle just came on the radio advertising a new McDonald's breakfast sandwich with a hollandaise-like sauce: The Benedict McMuffin. The spot also mentions a new hot ham and cheese sandwich. Bingo! This goes on all the time. And as these new products catch on, the old ones are moved aside to clog the big artery in the sky. These "Dead Foods," as I call them, include recent un-favorites such as McDonald's Arch Deluxe (page 123) and Burger King's Big King (page 26). They might be missing from menus, but I believe these products deserve a place to live here in this book. If you're one of the 12 fans of the Arch Deluxe, the only way you can take a little trip back in time to enjoy that same taste is to clone one of your own at home.

In addition to cloning dead foods, we can also clone the products that are only available at certain times of the year. Cadbury's Creme Egg (page 35) and Girl Scout Cookies (pages 62, 64) are good examples. Spring may be months away, but with the recipes in this book, you can now enjoy the taste of Thin Mints any time you want. And the cloned cookies will be even fresher than those you get in a box.

And what if you live in parts of the country where many of these products are unavailable? It's nearly impossible to find a fresh box of Drake's Devil Dogs (page 53) on the west coast. And just forget about wolfing down a hot Wienerschnitzel chili dog (page 202) if you live back east. Ah, but never fear, a clone recipe is here!

If you're new to these *Top Secret Recipes* books, and even if you aren't, let me now take some time to give you a few basic pointers that I've picked up along the way to help make your top secret cooking experience a dandy one. The recipes are designed with common ingredients and with as simple a process as I could muster, but since kitchen cloning is an inexact science, some thoughts come to mind:

• **Measure your ingredients very carefully.** These recipes copy products that are produced under highly controlled conditions. Although no two of you making these recipes at home will measure the ingredients exactly the same, you should still take the time to make accurate measurements with good measuring tools. Use liquid measuring cups (with the spouts) for the liquids, and dry measuring cups (no spouts) for the dry ingredients. Take time in measuring, never estimate, and resist the urge to make these recipes in a Winnebago kitchen while speeding down a dirt road in Tijuana.

• **Don't worry if your clone doesn't look exactly like the real thing.** Since many of these products are made by machines in custom molds and may include coloring or thickening additives that we won't use, your clone may look different from the real thing. That's okay. I usually try to include tricks to duplicate a product's appearance whenever possible (such as the foil mold for the Zingers clone, and various food colorings and consumer thickeners in other recipes). But my primary goal is to design a recipe that makes a finished product taste just like the real thing. Taste is job #1.

• **Use brand-name ingredients.** When I create these recipes I'm sure to use popular brands such as Best Foods Mayonnaise (or Hellmann's in the East), and Schilling, McCormick, and Spice Island spices. Generic brands may not be of the same quality and the final taste could be affected. For staple ingredients such as sugar, flour, and milk, you can use any old brand.

• **Don't be afraid to experiment.** The beauty of making Pay-Day candy bars at home is that we can make them twice as big! The joy of cooking KFC BBQ Baked Beans at home is that we can add more garlic and some kickin' cayenne pepper to our version! Tweak your recipes to suit your tastes. Use ground turkey in your hamburgers and top 'em with soy American cheese if you want. That's the best part of home clone cuisine. If you like to customize your food to create something you can't get in the stores, no one can stop you.

• **Have fun, man!** Cloning your own brand-name food at home is some of the most fun you'll have in the kitchen. Kids love it, adults dig it. And it's even more of a kick when you genuinely fool somebody with a food that they thought could only be bought in a restaurant or store. That's what makes cleaning up that big mess you just made worth all the trouble!

I hope you enjoy cooking from this book as much as I've enjoyed writing it. If you want more recipes like these, check out the other books in the *Top Secret Recipes* series. You'll also find plenty of recipes and handy cooking tips on the *Top Secret Recipes* Web site at: *www.TopSecretRecipes.com.*

If you have any suggestions for other recipes to clone, I'd love to see your e-mail:

Todd@TopSecretRecipes.com

Enjoy the book, and happy cloning!

EVEN MORE TOP SECRET RECIPES

ARBY'S
BRONCO BERRY SAUCE

☆　♥　☎　✎　✈　✉　✄　☛　✿

This sweet and spicy jelly sauce comes on the side, in little 1.5-ounce containers, with Arby's battered jalapeño and cheese Side Kickers. But, you know, you just never get enough of the tasty gelatinous goo in those little dipping packs to use later with your own home-cooked delicacies. And isn't it odd that the sauce is called "Bronco Berry" when there's not a berry to be found in there? Sure, the sauce is bright red and sugary, but you won't find a speck of fruit on the ingredients list. Nevertheless, the sweet and spicy flavors make this a delicious jelly sauce that has many uses beyond dipping quick service finger foods. For one, use it as a side sauce for your next batch of lamb chops rather than mint jelly. It would take more than just a few blister packs to perk up that meal.

¾ cup water
⅓ cup sugar
¼ cup corn syrup
3 tablespoons pectin
2 teaspoons cornstarch
1 teaspoon vinegar
50 drops or ¼ teaspoon red food coloring

⅛ teaspoon onion powder
dash cayenne pepper
dash garlic powder
dash paprika
¼ cup minced red bell pepper
½ teaspoon minced canned jalapeño peppers

1. Combine all the ingredients except the bell and minced jalapeño peppers in a small saucepan. Whisk well.

2. Set saucepan over medium/high heat, uncovered. Add peppers and bring mixture to a full boil, stirring often.
3. Reduce heat and simmer sauce for 5 to 7 minutes, or until thick. Remove from heat and let sauce sit for about 10 minutes. Stir and cover.
4. Use sauce when it reaches room temperature or cover and chill until needed.

• MAKES 1 CUP.

AUNTIE ANNE'S PRETZELS

☆   ♥   ☎   ✎   ✈   ✉   ✂   ☛   ✿

The first Auntie Anne's pretzel store opened in 1988 in the heart of pretzel country—a Pennsylvania Amish farmers' market. Over 500 stores later, Auntie Anne's is one of the most requested secret clone recipes around, especially on the Internet. Many of the recipes passed around the Web require bread flour, and some use honey as a sweetener. But by analyzing the Auntie Anne's home pretzel-making kit in the secret underground laboratory, I've discovered a better solution for re-creating the delicious mall treats than any clone recipe out there. For the best-quality dough, you just need all-purpose flour. And powdered sugar works great to perfectly sweeten the dough. Now you just have to decide if you want to make the more traditional salted pretzels, or the sweet cinnamon sugar–coated kind. Decisions, decisions.

1¼ cups warm water
1 tablespoon plus ¼ teaspoon yeast
3¾ cups all-purpose flour
¾ cup plus 2 tablespoons powdered sugar
1½ teaspoons salt
2 teaspoons vegetable oil

BATH
4 cups warm water

½ cup baking soda

¼ cup butter, melted

SALTED
kosher or pretzel salt

CINNAMON TOPPING
½ cup granulated sugar
2 teaspoons cinnamon

1. Dissolve the yeast in the warm water in a small bowl or cup. Let it sit for a few minutes.

2. Combine flour, powdered sugar, and salt in a large mixing bowl. Add water with yeast and vegetable oil. Stir with a spoon and then use your hands to form the dough into a ball. Knead the dough for 5 minutes on a lightly floured surface. Dough will be nice and smooth when it's ready. Place the dough into a lightly oiled bowl, cover it, and store it in a warm place for about 45 minutes or until the dough doubles in size.

3. When dough has risen, preheat oven to 425 degrees.

4. Make a bath for the pretzels by combining the baking soda with the warm water and stir until baking soda is mostly dissolved.

5. Remove the dough from the bowl and divide it into eight even portions. Roll each portion on a flat non-floured surface until it is about 3 feet long. Pick up both ends of the dough and give it a little spin so the middle of the dough spins around once. Lay the dough down with the loop nearest to you. Fold the ends down toward you and pinch to attach them to the bottom of the loop. The twist should be in the middle.

6. Holding the pinched ends, dip each pretzel into the bath solution. Put each pretzel on a paper towel for a moment to blot the excess liquid. Arrange the pretzels on a baking sheet sprayed with non-stick spray. If you want salt, sprinkle pretzels with kosher salt or pretzel salt. Don't salt any pretzels you plan to coat with cinnamon sugar. You will likely have to use two baking sheets, and be sure to bake them separately. Bake the pretzels for 4 minutes, then spin the pan halfway around and bake for another 4 to 5 minutes or until the pretzels are golden brown.

7. Remove the pretzels from the oven, and let them cool for a couple of minutes. If you want to eat some now, brush 'em with melted butter first, if desired, before serving. If you want the cinnamon sugar coating, make it by combining the ½ cup sugar and 2 teaspoons cinnamon in a small bowl. Brush the unsalted pretzels you plan to coat with a generous amount of

melted butter. Sprinkle a heavy coating of the cinnamon sugar onto the entire surface of the pretzels over a plate. Munch out.

- MAKES 8 PRETZELS.

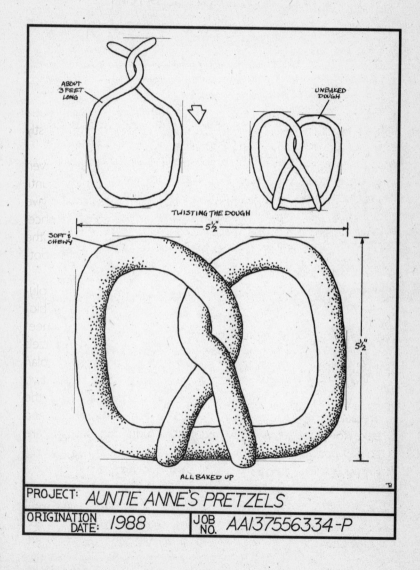

ABOUT 3 FEET LONG

UNBAKED DOUGH

TWISTING THE DOUGH

5½"

SOFT & CHEWY

5½"

ALL BAKED UP

PROJECT: AUNTIE ANNE'S PRETZELS

ORIGINATION DATE: 1988

JOB NO. AA137556334-P

BASKIN-ROBBINS
ICE CREAM CAKE

☆　　♥　　☎　　✎　　✈　　✉　　✂　　☛　　✿

Traditional white birthday cakes are pretty boring by themselves. Scoop a little ice cream onto the plate and I'll perk up a bit. But, hey baby, bring a Baskin-Robbins ice cream cake to the party and I'll be the first one in line with a plastic fork. This 4500-unit ice cream chain stacks several varieties of pre-made ice cream cakes in its freezer, but I've discovered the most popular version, over and over again, is the one made from white cake with pralines and cream ice cream on top. So that's got to be the version we clone here. But don't think you're locked into this formula—you can use any flavor of cake and ice cream you fancy for your homemade masterpiece. Just be sure the ice cream you choose comes in a box. It should be a rectangular shape so that the ice cream layer stacks up right. Then you'll want to find a real sharp serrated knife to cut the ice cream in half while it's still in the box. And check this out: That white stuff that coats the cake is actually softened ice cream spread on in a thin layer like frosting, and then re-frozen. After it sets up, you can decorate the cake any way you like with pre-made frosting in whatever color suits the festive occasion. Voilà! You've just made an ice cream cake at home that looks and tastes exactly like those in the stores that cost around 35 bucks each.

CAKE

1 box white cake mix
1¼ cups water

⅓ cup vegetable oil
3 egg whites

½-gallon box pralines and cream
   ice cream
4 cups (2 pints) vanilla ice cream
1 12-ounce container white frosting

OPTIONAL
colored frosting

1. Make your cake following the directions on the box. If you're making the white cake you'll likely blend the cake mix with water, oil, and 3 eggs. Pour the batter into a greased 9 × 13-inch baking pan and bake at 350 degrees for 30 to 35 minutes. This will make a thin cake for our bottom layer. When the cake is done, let it cool to room temperature.
2. When the cake has cooled, carefully remove it from the pan and place it onto a wax paper–covered cookie sheet, or a platter or tray that will fit into your freezer.
3. Use a sharp serrated knife (a bread knife works great) to slice the ice cream lengthwise through the middle, box and all, so that you have two 2-inch-thick sheets of ice cream. Peel the cardboard off the ice cream and lay the halves next to each other on the cake. Slice the edges of the cake all the way around so that the cake is the same size as the ice cream on top. Work quickly so that the ice cream doesn't melt. When the cake has been trimmed, place it into the freezer for an hour or two.
4. When you are ready to frost the cake, take the 2 pints (4 cups) of vanilla ice cream out of the freezer for 20 to 30 minutes to soften. Stir the ice cream so that it is smooth, like frosting. Use a frosting knife or spatula to coat your cake with about 2 cups of ice cream. Cover the entire surface thoroughly so that you cannot see any of the cake or ice cream underneath. Pop the cake into the freezer for an hour or so to set up.
5. When the cake has set, fill a pastry bag (with a fancy tip) with white frosting to decorate all around the top edge of the cake. Also decorate around the bottom of the cake. Use colored frosting and different tips to add inspired artistic flair and

writing on the cake, as needed. Cover the cake with plastic wrap and keep it in your freezer until party time.

6. When you are ready to serve the cake, leave it out for 10 minutes before slicing. Cut the cake with a sharp knife that has been held under hot water.

• MAKES 1 LARGE CAKE (16–20 SERVINGS).

TIDBITS

You may wish to use another flavor cake mix such as chocolate or devil's food for this dessert—even low-fat cake mix works. It's up to you. Just follow the directions on the box for making the cake in a 9×13-inch baking pan.

You can also use any flavor of ice cream. Just be sure to get it in a box.

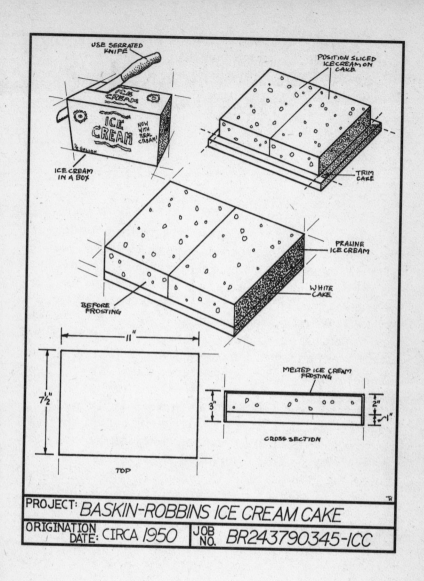

USE SERRATED KNIFE

POSITION SLICED ICE CREAM ON CAKE

ICE CREAM IN A BOX

TRIM CAKE

PRALINE ICE CREAM

WHITE CAKE

BEFORE FROSTING

11"

7½"

TOP

MELTED ICE CREAM FROSTING

3"

2"

1"

CROSS SECTION

PROJECT: BASKIN-ROBBINS ICE CREAM CAKE

ORIGINATION DATE: CIRCA 1950

JOB NO. BR243790345-ICC

BOSTON MARKET
MEATLOAF

☆　♥　☎　✎　✈　⊠　✄　☞　✿

In the early 90s Boston Chicken was on a roll. The home meal replacement chain's stock was soaring and the lines were filled with hungry customers waiting to sink their teeth into a serving of the chain's delicious rotisserie chicken. So successful was the chain with chicken, that the company quickly decided it was time to introduce other entrée selections, the first of which was a delicious barbecue sauce–covered ground sirloin meatloaf. But offering other entrées presented the company with a dilemma: what to do about the name. The bigwigs decided it was time to change the name to Boston Market, to reflect a wider menu. That meant replacing signs on hundreds of units and retooling the marketing campaigns. That name change, plus rapid expansion of the chain and growth of other similar home-style meal concepts sent the company into a tailspin. By 1998, Boston Market's goose was cooked: the company filed for bankruptcy. Soon McDonald's stepped in to purchase the company, with the idea of closing many of the stores for good, and slapping Golden Arches on the rest. But that plan was scrapped when, after selling off many of the under-performing Boston Markets, the chain began to fly once again. Within a year of the acquisition Boston Market was profitable, and those meals with the home-cooked taste are still being served at over 700 Boston Market restaurants across the country.

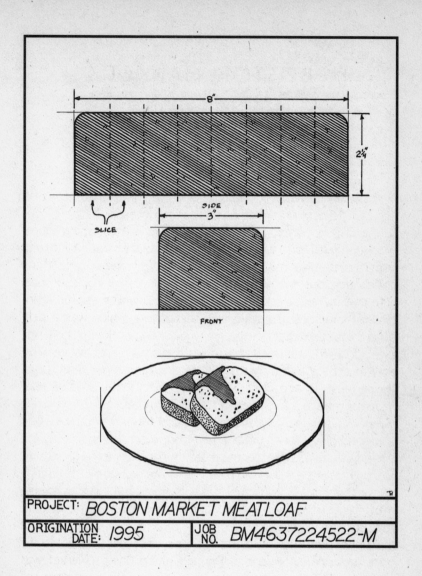

8"

2¼"

SLICE

SIDE
3"

FRONT

PROJECT: *BOSTON MARKET MEATLOAF*

ORIGINATION
DATE: *1995*

JOB
NO. *BM4637224522-M*

23

1 cup tomato sauce
1 ½ tablespoons Kraft original barbecue sauce
1 tablespoon granulated sugar
1 ½ pounds ground sirloin (10 percent fat)

6 tablespoons all-purpose flour
¾ teaspoon salt
½ teaspoon onion powder
¼ teaspoon ground black pepper
dash garlic powder

1. Preheat oven to 400 degrees.
2. Combine the tomato sauce, barbecue sauce, and sugar in a small saucepan over medium heat. Heat the mixture until it begins to bubble, stirring often, then remove it from the heat.
3. In a large bowl, add all but 2 tablespoons of the tomato sauce to the meat. Use a large wooden spoon or your hands to work the sauce into the meat until it is very well combined.
4. Combine the remaining ingredients with the ground sirloin—flour, salt, onion powder, ground pepper, and garlic powder. Use the wooden spoon or your hands to work the spices and flour into the meat.
5. Load the meat into a loaf pan (preferably a meatloaf pan with two sections that allows the fat to drain, but if you don't have one of those a regular loaf pan will work). Wrap foil over the pan and place it into the oven for 30 minutes.
6. After 30 minutes, take the meatloaf from the oven, remove the foil and, if you aren't using a meatloaf pan, drain the fat.
7. Using a knife, slice the meatloaf all the way through into 8 slices while it is still in the pan. This will help to cook the center of the meatloaf. Pour the remaining 2 tablespoons of sauce over the top of the meatloaf, in a stream down the center. Don't spread the sauce.
8. Place the meatloaf back into the oven, uncovered, for 25 to 30 minutes or until it is done. Remove and allow it to cool for a few minutes before serving.

• SERVES 4.

BULL'S-EYE
ORIGINAL BBQ SAUCE

☆　♥　☎　✎　✈　✉　✂　☞　✿

Some say it's the best off-the-shelf barbecue sauce in the business. That secret combination of molasses, liquid smoke, and spices makes this stuff irresistible on chicken, ribs, or juicy hamburger. If it's grilling time and you're all out of sauce, why not whip up a clone batch of your own when it's this friggin' easy?

1 cup water
¾ cup light corn syrup
½ cup tomato paste
⅔ cup vinegar
⅓ cup dark brown sugar
3 tablespoons molasses
1 ¼ teaspoons liquid smoke (see
　Tidbits)

1 teaspoon salt
¼ teaspoon onion powder
¼ teaspoon ground black pepper
¼ teaspoon ground mustard
⅛ teaspoon paprika
⅛ teaspoon garlic powder
dash cayenne pepper

1. Combine all ingredients in a medium saucepan over high heat and whisk until smooth.
2. Bring mixture to a boil, then reduce heat and simmer uncovered for 45 minutes or until thick.
3. Cool, then store in a covered container in the refrigerator overnight.

• MAKES 1 ½ CUPS.

TIDBITS

Liquid smoke is a flavoring found near the barbecue sauces and marinades. Use hickory-flavored liquid smoke if you have a choice.

BURGER KING
BIG KING

☆ ♥ ☎ ✎ ✈ ✉ ✂ ☞ ✿

The Burger Wars have become the biggest food fight since that cafeteria scene from the movie *Animal House*. The two burger giants, McDonald's and Burger King, have each been cloning the other's top products in the bloody battle for the big burger buck. Burger King stepped up first with the Big King—Burger King's version of McDonald's Big Mac. Yes, it had two all-beef patties, special sauce, lettuce, cheese, pickles, onions on a sesame seed bun; although everything was arranged a bit differently, and there's no middle bun in there. Then McDonald's rolled out the Big 'N Tasty, which bore a striking resemblance to Burger King's Whopper, with fresh lettuce, tomato, and onion on top of a huge beef patty (find a clone recipe for this one on page 126). Who's winning this fight by leveraging the popularity of the other company's product? Nobody, really. McDonald's chose to alter its Big 'N Tasty recipe by making it smaller 'n cheaper, then changed the name to BigXtra!, while Burger King limited sale of the Big King. But this food fight is far from over. More recently Burger King tweaked its french fry formula in an unsuccessful attempt to steal away fans of McDonald's winning fried spuds recipe. And McDonald's has added more breakfast sandwiches to compete with Burger King's wider wake-up selection. So the war continues. And the battlefield is splattered with ketchup.

1 ½ pounds ground beef
dash salt
dash pepper
4 sesame seed hamburger buns
1 ⅓ cups chopped lettuce
8 slices American cheese
1 to 2 slices white onion,
   separated
8 dill pickle slices

SPREAD
¼ cup mayonnaise
2 teaspoons French dressing
2 teaspoons sweet pickle relish
1 teaspoon white vinegar
½ teaspoon sugar
¼ teaspoon lemon juice
⅛ teaspoon paprika

1. Prepare the spread by combining the ingredients in a small bowl. Set this aside until you are ready to use it.
2. Preheat your barbecue or indoor grill to high heat.
3. Divide the ground beef into eight even portions (3 ounces each). Roll each portion into a ball, then press each ball flat to form a patty about the same diameter as the bun.
4. Grill the beef patties for 2 to 3 minutes per side, or until done. Lightly salt and pepper each side of the patties.
5. As the meat cooks, brown the faces of the buns in a hot skillet, toaster oven, or facedown on the grill. Watch the buns closely so that they do not burn.
6. Build each burger by first spreading a tablespoon of the spread on the face of the top bun. Arrange about ⅓ cup of lettuce evenly over the spread.
7. On the bottom bun stack a patty, then a slice of American cheese, another patty, and another slice of cheese.
8. On the top slice of cheese arrange 2 to 3 separated onion slices (rings), then 2 pickle slices.
9. Turn the top part of the burger over onto the bottom and serve. You may also want to zap the sandwiches in the microwave, individually, for 15 to 20 seconds each.

• SERVES 4.

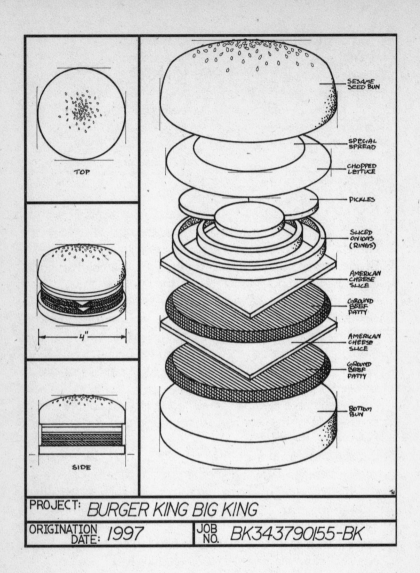

TOP

4"

SIDE

SESAME
SEED BUN

SPECIAL
SPREAD

CHOPPED
LETTUCE

PICKLES

SLICED
ONIONS
(RINGS)

AMERICAN
CHEESE
SLICE

GROUND
BEEF
PATTY

AMERICAN
CHEESE
SLICE

GROUND
BEEF
PATTY

BOTTOM
BUN

PROJECT: *BURGER KING BIG KING*

ORIGINATION
DATE: *1997*

JOB
NO. *BK343790155-BK*

BURGER KING
BK BROILER

☆　　❤　　☎　　✎　　✈　　✉　　✂　　☛　　✿

This grilled chicken sandwich was introduced by America's number-two burger chain in 1990, and soon after the launch the BK Broiler was selling at a rate of over a million a day. Not good news for chickens.

This one's easy to duplicate at home. To clone the shape of the chicken served at the burger giant, you'll simply slice the chicken breasts in half, and pound each piece flat with a mallet. Pounding things is fun. Let the chicken marinate and then fire up the grill. The recipe makes four sandwiches and can be easily doubled if necessary for a king-size munch-fest.

MARINADE

¾ cup water

2 teaspoons ketchup

1 teaspoon salt

¼ teaspoon liquid smoke (see Tidbits on page 25)

⅛ teaspoon pepper

⅛ teaspoon oregano

dash onion powder

dash parsley

2 skinless chicken breast fillets

4 sesame seed hamburger buns

1⅓ cups chopped lettuce

¼ cup mayonnaise

8 tomato slices

1. Make the marinade by combining the ingredients in a medium bowl.
2. Prepare the chicken by cutting each breast in half. Fold a piece of plastic wrap around each piece of chicken and pound the meat with a tenderizing mallet until it is about ¼-inch thick and about the same diameter as the hamburger buns. Place

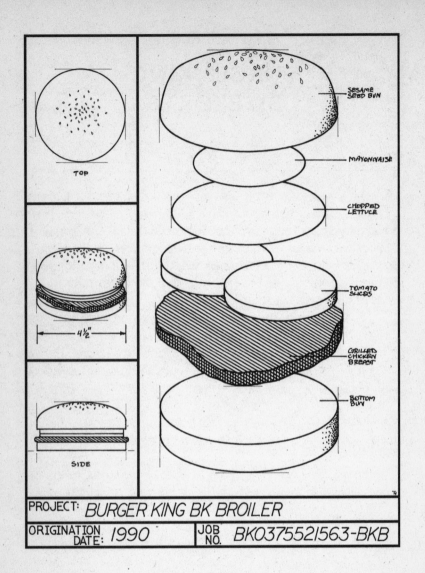

TOP

SIDE

4½"

SESAME
SEED BUN

MAYONNAISE

CHOPPED
LETTUCE

TOMATO
SLICES

GRILLED
CHICKEN
BREAST

BOTTOM
BUN

PROJECT: *BURGER KING BK BROILER*

ORIGINATION
DATE: *1990*

JOB
NO. *BK037552I563-BKB*

the chicken into the marinade, cover it, and chill for at least 4 hours. Overnight is even better.

3. Preheat your barbecue or indoor grill to high heat. Grill the chicken for 3 to 4 minutes per side or until done.

4. Toast the faces of the hamburger buns in a pan or griddle, in a toaster oven, or facedown on the grill. Watch the buns closely to be certain that the faces turn only light brown and do not burn.

5. Build each sandwich from the top down by first spreading about a tablespoon of the mayonnaise on the toasted face of a top bun.

6. Spread about 1/3 cup of chopped lettuce over the mayonnaise.

7. Arrange two tomato slices on the lettuce.

8. Place a chicken breast on the toasted face of the bottom bun.

9. Flip the top part of the sandwich over onto the bottom and scarf out.

- SERVES 4.

BURGER KING
BREAKFAST SANDWICHES

☆　♥　☎　✎　✈　✉　✂　☛　❀

Get vertical with these top secret breakfasts-in-sandwich from the world's number-two fast food chain. A great way to make the eggs for these breakfast sandwiches is to pour the beaten egg into a well-greased mold made from an empty pineapple can. Just cut both ends off an 8-ounce pineapple can—you know, the short cans that have the crushed or sliced pineapple inside. Oh, and take the pineapple out. Then, before you know it, you'll be making perfectly round eggs like the fast food pros.

BISCUIT SANDWICH

1 small can (5 biscuits) Pillsbury
   Grands Buttermilk Biscuits
melted butter
non-stick cooking spray
5 eggs
salt

ground black pepper
10 ounces ground breakfast
   sausage (such as Jimmy Dean)
   or 10 slices of bacon
5 slices American cheese

1. Prepare biscuits following instructions on the can (bake at 350 degrees for 15 to 18 minutes). When you remove the biscuits from the oven brush the top of each with melted butter.
2. Spray a skillet over medium heat with non-stick cooking spray. Open both ends of a clean, small, sliced pineapple can. Spray the inside of the empty can with the non-stick spray, and then place the can in the pan to heat up. Use more than one can if you'd like to speed up the cooking process.

3. Beat an egg, then pour it into the empty can mold, add a bit of salt and pepper, and cover with a saucepan lid. Cook for a couple minutes, then scrape a knife around the edge of the egg to release it. Remove the can, then turn the egg over and cook it for another minute or 2. Repeat with the remaining eggs.

4. If using sausage, form 2-ounce portions of sausage into patties with the same diameter as the biscuits. Cook the sausage in another hot skillet over medium heat until brown. If using bacon, cook the bacon and drain on paper towels.

5. Slice a biscuit in half through the middle. Build each sandwich by first stacking egg on the bottom half of the biscuit. Next arrange sausage (or 2 slices of bacon) on the egg, then a slice of American cheese. Top off each sandwich with the top biscuit half, and then zap it in the microwave for 15 to 20 seconds to help melt the cheese. Repeat with the remaining ingredients.

• MAKES 5 SANDWICHES.

CROISSAN'WICH

1 8-ounce can Pillsbury Original
    Crescent Rolls
4 eggs
salt
ground black pepper

8 ounces ground breakfast
    sausage (such as Jimmy Dean)
    or 8 slices bacon
4 slices American cheese

1. Prepare the rolls by first unrolling the dough out of the can. Separate the dough into four sections, each made up of two triangles. Detach the triangles by tearing along the diagonal perforation, then reattach the dough along the outside parallel edges, pinching the dough together along the middle. This will make one bigger triangle. Loosely roll the dough, starting from the wide end, all the way up. Now, bring the ends around so that they overlap and the roll is in the shape of a circle. Press the ends together and place the roll onto a baking sheet. Repeat with the remaining dough, then bake following the directions on the package (bake at 375 degrees for 11 to 13 minutes).

2. When the rolls are done baking build the sandwich using steps 2 through 5 in the recipe for the biscuit sandwich clone.
- MAKES 4 SANDWICHES.

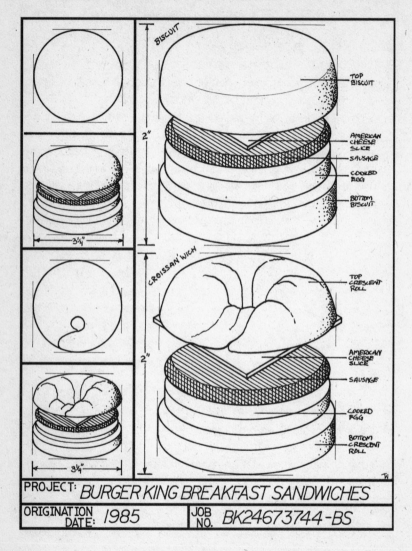

PROJECT: BURGER KING BREAKFAST SANDWICHES

ORIGINATION DATE: 1985

JOB NO. BK24673744-BS

CADBURY'S
CREME EGG

☆　♥　☎　✎　✈　✉　✂　☛　✿

Here's a way to get your Easter candy fix, even when it's not Easter-time. It's a clone version of the first soft fondant-filled egg candy to hit the market many Easters ago. Each spring Cadbury candy machines whip out 66,000 of these cool candies every hour. And now, because of the success of these chocolates with the orange, yolk-colored center, other candy companies have come out with their own milk chocolate eggs. Some are filled with Snickers or Milky Way centers, while others contain peanut butter, coconut, caramel, or the same type of fondant center as the original ... right down to the colors. Still, nothing compares with the original eggs that are sold only once a year, for the Easter holiday. Enjoy your own version at home anytime you like. With this recipe that won't require you to make anything close to 66,000 of 'em.

½ cup light corn syrup
¼ cup butter, softened
1 teaspoon vanilla
¼ teaspoon salt
3 cups powdered sugar
4 drops yellow food coloring

2 drops red food coloring
1 12-ounce bag milk chocolate chips
2 tablespoons vegetable shortening

1. Combine the corn syrup, butter, vanilla, and salt in a large bowl. Beat well with an electric mixer until smooth.
2. Add powdered sugar, one cup at a time, mixing by hand after each addition. Mix well until creamy.

3. Remove about ⅓ of the mixture and place it into a small bowl. Add the yellow and red food coloring and stir well to combine.

4. Cover both mixtures and refrigerate for at least 2 hours, or until firm.

5. When mixtures are firm, roll a small, marble-size ball from the orange filling, and wrap a portion of the white filling around it that is roughly twice the size. Form this filling into the shape of an egg and place it onto a cookie sheet that has been brushed with a light coating of shortening. Repeat for the remaining filling ingredients, then refrigerate these centers for 3 to 4 hours or until firm.

6. Combine the milk chocolate chips with the shortening in a glass or ceramic bowl. Microwave chocolate on high speed for 1 minute, then stir gently and microwave again for 1 more minute, and stir gently. Be very careful not to overcook the chocolate or it could seize up on you and become unusable.

7. Use a fork to dip each center into the chocolate, tap the fork on the side of the bowl, then place each candy onto wax paper. Chill.

8. After 1 to 2 hours of chilling, dip each candy once more and chill for several hours, or until completely firm.

• MAKES 2 DOZEN CANDY EGGS.

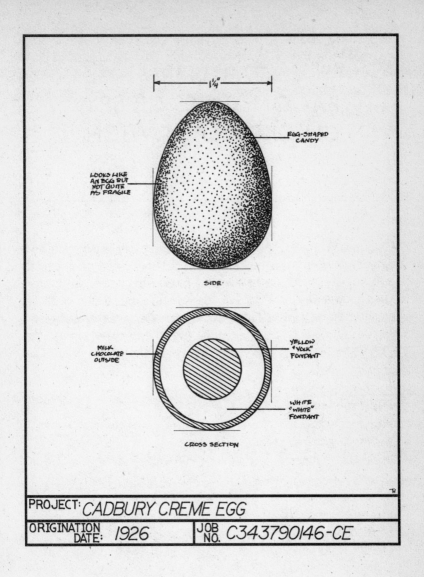

1¼"

EGG-SHAPED
CANDY

LOOKS LIKE
AN EGG BUT
NOT QUITE
AS FRAGILE

SIDE

MILK
CHOCOLATE
OUTSIDE

YELLOW
"YOLK"
FONDANT

WHITE
"WHITE"
FONDANT

CROSS SECTION

PROJECT: CADBURY CREME EGG	
ORIGINATION DATE: 1926	JOB NO. C343790146-CE

CARL'S JR.
BACON SWISS CRISPY
CHICKEN SANDWICH

☆   ♥   ☎   ✎   ✈   ✉   ✂   ☞   ❀

If you love crispy chicken sandwiches—and especially if you don't live in the West—you'll want to try out this clone of the tasty Carl's Jr. creation. The recipe makes four of the addicting chicken sandwiches from the California-based chain, but will also come in handy for making a delicious homemade ranch dressing. Try using some lean turkey bacon, fat-free Swiss cheese, and light mayonnaise if you feel like cutting back on the fat. Then you can eat two.

RANCH DRESSING

⅓ cup mayonnaise

2 tablespoons sour cream

1 tablespoon buttermilk

1½ teaspoons white vinegar

1 teaspoon sugar

¼ teaspoon lemon juice

⅛ teaspoon salt

⅛ teaspoon parsley

⅛ teaspoon onion powder

dash dill weed

dash garlic powder

dash ground black pepper

2 teaspoons hot water

½ teaspoon unflavored gelatin

6 to 8 cups vegetable shortening

1 egg

1 cup water

1 cup all-purpose flour

2½ teaspoons salt

1 teaspoon paprika

1 teaspoon onion powder

⅛ teaspoon garlic powder

4 skinless chicken breast fillets

4 sesame seed hamburger buns

4 lettuce leaves

4 tomato slices

Kraft Singles Swiss cheese

8 slices bacon, cooked

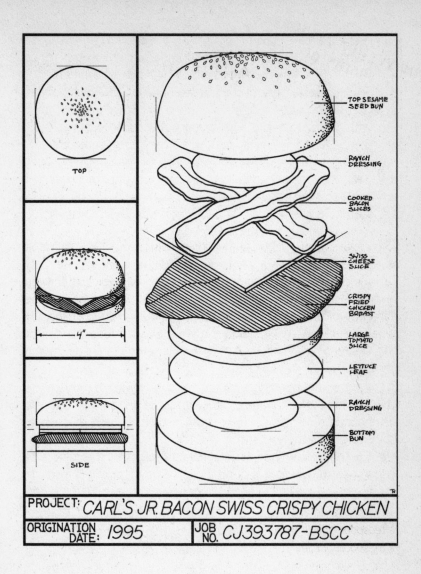

TOP

4"

SIDE

TOP SESAME
SEED BUN

RANCH
DRESSING

COOKED
BACON
SLICES

SWISS
CHEESE
SLICE

CRISPY
FRIED
CHICKEN
BREAST

LARGE
TOMATO
SLICE

LETTUCE
LEAF

RANCH
DRESSING

BOTTOM
BUN

PROJECT: *CARL'S JR. BACON SWISS CRISPY CHICKEN*

ORIGINATION
DATE: *1995*

JOB
NO. *CJ393787-BSCC*

1. Preheat 6 to 8 cups of shortening in a deep fryer to 350 degrees. If you don't have a deep fryer, you can also pan fry using a large frying pan and just a couple cups of shortening.
2. To prepare the ranch dressing, combine all of the ingredients except the water and gelatin in a small bowl. Mix the water with the gelatin in a small cup until all of the gelatin is dissolved. Add this gelatin solution to the other ingredients and stir. Cover and chill the dressing until it's needed.
3. Beat the egg and then combine with 1 cup of water in a small, shallow bowl. Stir.
4. Combine the flour, salt, paprika, onion powder, and garlic powder in another shallow bowl.
5. Pound each of the breast fillets with a mallet until about ¼-inch thick. Trim each breast fillet until it is round.
6. Working with one fillet at a time, first coat each fillet with the flour, then dredge it in the egg and water mixture. Coat the chicken once again in the flour and set it aside until all of the fillets have been coated.
7. Fry the chicken fillets for 8 to 12 minutes or until light brown and crispy.
8. As chicken is frying, prepare each sandwich by grilling the face of the hamburger buns on a hot skillet over medium heat. Spread about 1½ teaspoons of the ranch dressing on the face of the top and bottom buns.
9. On the bottom bun, stack a leaf of lettuce and a tomato slice.
10. When the chicken is done frying, remove the fillets from the fryer and drain them on paper towels or a rack for a couple minutes.
11. Stack one fillet on the bottom of the sandwich (on top of the tomato), then stack a slice of the Swiss cheese onto the chicken.
12. Arrange the bacon, crosswise, on top of the Swiss cheese, then top off the sandwich with the top bun. Repeat the stacking process for each of the remaining sandwiches.

• MAKES 4 SANDWICHES.

CARL'S JR.
RANCH CRISPY CHICKEN SANDWICH

☆ ♥ ☎ ✎ ✈ ✉ ✂ ☛ ✿

We'll use elements of the previous recipe to whip up another one of Carl's Jr's crispy chicken sandwiches, because I always say you can never have too much crispy chicken. This fried chicken breast sandwich includes lettuce and tomato, and is slathered with a clone of Carl's tasty ranch dressing. Use the recipes together and you can easily serve up two different sandwich clones for different tastes, with little extra effort. And your diners will be so impressed.

RANCH DRESSING

⅓ cup mayonnaise

2 tablespoons sour cream

1 tablespoon buttermilk

1½ teaspoons white vinegar

1 teaspoon sugar

¼ teaspoon lemon juice

⅛ teaspoon salt

⅛ teaspoon parsley

⅛ teaspoon onion powder

dash dill weed

dash garlic powder

dash ground black pepper

2 teaspoons hot water

½ teaspoon unflavored gelatin

6 to 8 cups vegetable shortening

1 egg

1 cup water

1 cup all-purpose flour

2½ teaspoons salt

1 teaspoon paprika

1 teaspoon onion powder

⅛ teaspoon garlic powder

4 skinless chicken breast fillets

4 sesame seed hamburger buns

4 lettuce leaves

4 tomato slices

1. Preheat 6 to 8 cups of oil in a deep fryer to 350 degrees. If you don't have a deep fryer, you can also pan fry using a large frying pan, and just a couple cups of shortening.
2. To prepare the ranch dressing, combine all of the ingredients except the water and gelatin in a small bowl. Mix the water with the gelatin in a small cup until all of the gelatin is dissolved. Add this gelatin solution to the other ingredients and stir. Cover and chill the dressing until it's needed.
3. Beat the egg and then combine with 1 cup of water in a small, shallow bowl. Stir.
4. Combine the flour, salt, paprika, onion powder, and garlic powder in another shallow bowl.
5. Pound each of the breast fillets with a mallet until about 1/4-inch thick. Trim each breast fillet until it is round.
6. Working with one fillet at a time, first coat each fillet with the flour, then dredge it in the egg and water mixture. Coat the chicken once again in the flour and set it aside until all of the fillets have been coated.
7. Fry the chicken fillets for 8 to 12 minutes or until light brown and crispy.
8. As the chicken is frying, prepare each sandwich by grilling the face of the hamburger buns on a hot skillet over medium heat. Spread about 1½ teaspoons of the ranch dressing on the face of the top and bottom buns.
9. On the bottom bun, stack a leaf of lettuce and a tomato slice.
10. When the chicken is done frying, remove the fillets from the fryer and drain on paper towels or a rack for a couple minutes.
11. Stack one fillet on the bottom of the sandwich (on top of the tomato), then top it off with the top bun. Repeat the stacking process for each of the sandwiches.

• MAKES 4 SANDWICHES.

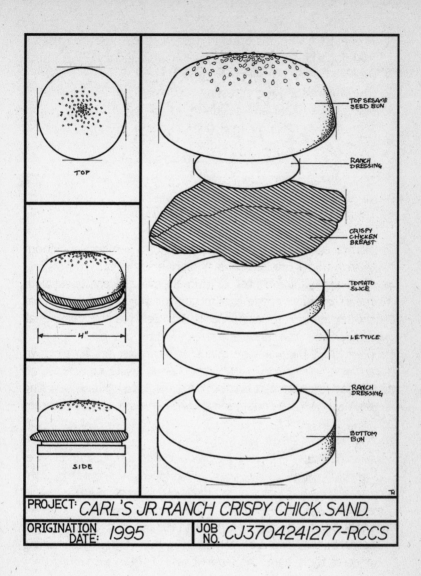

TOP

4"

SIDE

TOP SESAME
SEED BUN

RANCH
DRESSING

CRISPY
CHICKEN
BREAST

TOMATO
SLICE

LETTUCE

RANCH
DRESSING

BOTTOM
BUN

PROJECT: *CARL'S JR. RANCH CRISPY CHICK. SAND.*

ORIGINATION DATE: *1995*

JOB NO. *CJ3704241277-RCCS*

43

CHEF PAUL PRUDHOMME'S POULTRY MAGIC

☆ ♥ ☎ ✎ ✈ ✉ ✄ ☞ ✿

Louisiana chef Paul Prudhomme, America's number one Dom DeLuise lookalike, hit it big in supermarkets with his magical brand of Cajun spice blends. Chef Paul developed his seasonings after years of making little batches and passing them out to customers in the restaurants where he worked. Now his Magic Seasoning Blends come in several varieties and are produced in a whopping 30,000-square-foot plant by 38 employees. Fortunately, it'll take only one of you in a small kitchen to make a clone of one of the most popular versions of the blend. Use it when you barbecue, roast, grill, or sauté your favorite chicken, turkey, duck, or Cornish game hens.

1 ½ teaspoons salt
½ teaspoon paprika
¼ teaspoon cayenne
¼ teaspoon onion powder
¼ teaspoon garlic powder

¼ teaspoon ground black pepper
¼ teaspoon dried thyme
¼ teaspoon dried oregano
¼ teaspoon rubbed sage
dash cumin

Combine all ingredients in a small bowl. Store in a covered container. Sprinkle on any poultry to taste.

• MAKES 4 TEASPOONS.

CINNABON CINNABONSTIX

☆ ♥ ☎ ✎ ✈ ✉ ✂ ☛ ✿

Cinnabon product development guys were looking for a new baked cinnamon product that customers could eat on the go while carrying bags and scurrying about. In June of 2000, they found it. Bakers brushed Danish dough with a flavored cinnamon butter, and then rolled the dough in a generous cinnamon sugar coating. These golden brown little sticks of cinnamony delight are sold in bags of five or ten from the company's famous cinnamon roll outlets, most likely found in a mall or airport near you. Now you can create your own version of the tasty pastries at home, and you won't even have to make the dough from scratch. Just grab yourself a tube of Pillsbury crescents and all you have to do is fold and roll up the dough, and then coat it. Run around the house in a hurry while eating these to further re-create the experience.

1 tube Pillsbury crescent dinner
   rolls (8)
1 stick (½ cup) margarine,
   melted
2 teaspoons granulated sugar
¼ teaspoon cinnamon

¼ teaspoon vanilla
non-stick cooking spray

COATING
½ cup granulated sugar
1 tablespoon cinnamon

1. Preheat oven to 400 degrees.
2. Separate the dough into eight portions. Fold over two of the corners of the triangular dough piece so that it forms a rectangle. Roll the dough on a flat surface to make a tube, then twist

the tube a couple of times, and stretch it a little longer. Repeat for all the dough triangles.

3. Combine the melted margarine, 2 teaspoons sugar, ¼ teaspoon cinnamon, and ¼ teaspoon vanilla in a small bowl.

4. Combine ½ cup sugar and 1 tablespoon cinnamon for the coating in another small bowl.

5. Brush the melted margarine mixture over the top and bottom of the dough sticks. Toss the dough into the sugar and cinnamon coating mixture. Roll the dough around with your fingers so that it is well coated. Place the coated dough sticks on a cookie sheet that has been sprayed with non-stick cooking spray. Spray the top of the sticks with a light coating of the spray.

6. Bake for 8 minutes or until the sticks are golden brown. Serve the sticks right out of the oven or reheat them in the microwave for just a bit before serving if they have cooled. These puppies are best served hot!

• MAKES 8 STICKS.

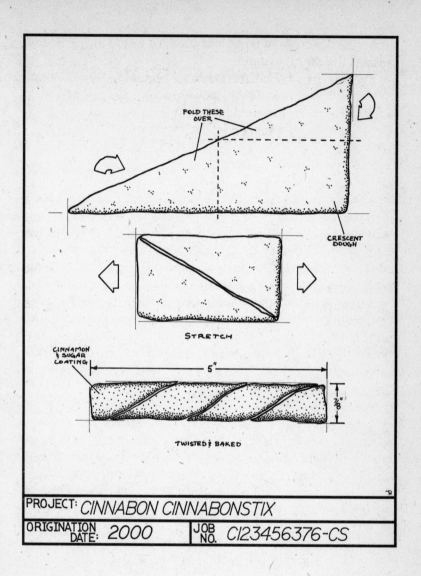

FOLD THESE OVER

CRESCENT DOUGH

STRETCH

CINNAMON & SUGAR COATING

5"

⅞"

TWISTED & BAKED

PROJECT: *CINNABON CINNABONSTIX*

ORIGINATION DATE: *2000*

JOB NO. *CI23456376-CS*

DOLLY MADISON ZINGERS (DEVIL'S FOOD)

☆ ♥ ☎ ✎ ✈ ✉ ✂ ☞ ✿

Former U.S. president James Madison's wife did not create this baking company, despite the fact that her name is on every carrot cake, crumb cake, and Zinger that comes off the production line. It was instead company founder Roy Nafziger's brainstorm to use the former first lady's name, since she was notorious for throwing huge shindigs featuring a fine selection of desserts and baked goods. Nafziger said his company would create cakes "fine enough to serve at the White House." While I don't expect you'll be treated to a tray of Zingers on your next stay in the Lincoln Bedroom, I will agree that these little snack cakes are a tasty way to appease a sweet tooth.

The cake batter is easy, since you just use any instant devil's food cake mix. I like Duncan Hines. As for the frosting, it may not come out as dark brown as the original since the recipe here doesn't include brown food coloring (caramel coloring). But the taste will be right on. And I think former president Clinton would agree that as long as the sweet little treats taste good, appearance is secondary.

CAKE
Duncan Hines devil's food cake mix
1⅓ cups water
½ cup oil
3 large eggs

FILLING
2 teaspoons hot water
¼ teaspoon salt
2 cups marshmallow creme (one 7-ounce jar)
½ cup shortening
⅓ cup powdered sugar
½ teaspoon vanilla

FROSTING
I cup powdered sugar
¼ cup Hershey's chocolate syrup

2 tablespoons shortening
½ teaspoon vanilla
dash salt

1. Prepare the cake batter following the directions on the box. If you use Duncan Hines brand, you will need 1⅓ cups of water, ½ cup of oil, and 3 eggs. Preheat oven to 350 degrees.
2. To prepare the cake pans that will make cakes the size of Zingers, tear off 20 pieces of aluminum foil that are each about 8 inches wide. Fold the foil in half and then in half once more so that you have a rectangular piece of foil. Wrap this piece of foil around a small prescription medicine bottle. Tuck in the ends and take the bottle out, leaving the foil open at the top. This will form a little pan. Flatten the bottom so that the mini pan stands up straight. Place this into a baking pan and repeat with the remaining pieces of foil. When you have arranged all of the foil pans in a baking pan, spray the inside of all the pans with non-stick cooking spray. Fill each little pan about halfway with cake batter. Bake cakes for 15 to 17 minutes or until a toothpick stuck in the center comes out clean. Remove the cakes from the oven and allow them to cool completely.
3. To make the filling, combine the hot water with the salt in a small bowl and stir until the salt is dissolved. Let this mixture cool.
4. Combine the marshmallow creme, shortening, powdered sugar, and vanilla in a medium bowl and mix well with an electric mixer on high speed until fluffy. Add the salt mixture to the bowl and mix.
5. To make the chocolate frosting, combine all the frosting ingredients in a medium bowl and mix well with an electric mixer until smooth.
6. To assemble your snack cakes first poke three holes with a toothpick or skewer in the top of a cake and swirl around inside the holes, making little caverns for your filling.
7. Use a pastry bag with a small tip to squeeze some filling into each hole. Careful not to overfill, or your cake will burst open. Sure, it looks cool when they explode, but this mess won't make for a very good clone.

8. Once the cake is filled, use a butter knife to spread frosting on top of the cake over the holes, concealing your secret injection work. Drag a fork lengthwise over the frosting, making grooves just like the real thing.
- MAKES 20 SNACK CAKES.

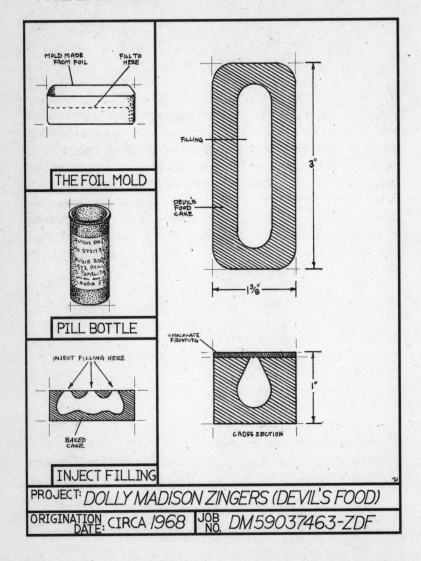

THE FOIL MOLD

PILL BOTTLE

INJECT FILLING

PROJECT: DOLLY MADISON ZINGERS (DEVIL'S FOOD)

ORIGINATION DATE: CIRCA 1968   JOB NO. DM59037463-ZDF

DOUBLETREE
CHOCOLATE CHIP COOKIES

☆　♥　☎　✎　✈　✉　✂　☛　❀

When you check in at one of 240 hotels run by this U.S. chain, you are handed a bag from a warming oven that contains two soft and delicious chocolate chip cookies. This is a tradition that began in the early 90s using a recipe from a small bakery in Atlanta. All of the cookies—which weigh in at an impressive two ounces each—are baked fresh every day on the hotel premises. Raves for the cookies from customers convinced the hotel chain to start selling the chocolatey munchables by the half-dozen. But if you've got an insatiable chocolate chip cookie urge that can't wait for a package to be delivered in the mail, you'll want to try this cloned version fresh out of your home oven.

½ cup rolled oats
2¼ cups all-purpose flour
1½ teaspoons baking soda
1 teaspoon salt
¼ teaspoon cinnamon
1 cup (2 sticks) butter, softened
¾ cup brown sugar, packed

¾ cup granulated sugar
1½ teaspoons vanilla
½ teaspoon lemon juice
2 eggs
3 cups semi-sweet chocolate
　chips
1½ cups chopped walnuts

1. Preheat oven to 350 degrees.
2. Grind oats in a food processor or blender until fine. Combine the ground oats with the flour, baking soda, salt, and cinnamon in a medium bowl.
3. Cream together the butter, sugars, vanilla, and lemon juice in another medium bowl with an electric mixer. Add the eggs and mix until smooth.

4. Stir the dry mixture into the wet mixture and blend well. Add the chocolate chips and nuts to the dough and mix by hand until ingredients are well incorporated.

5. Spoon rounded ¼-cup portions onto an ungreased cookie sheet. Place the scoops about 2 inches apart. You don't need to press the dough flat. Bake for 16 to 18 minutes or until cookies are light brown and soft in the middle. Store in a sealed container when cool to keep soft.

- MAKES 20 COOKIES.

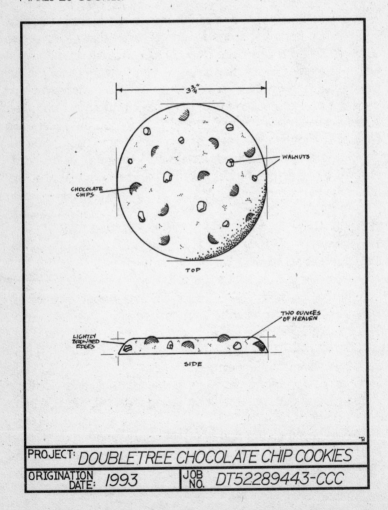

PROJECT: DOUBLETREE CHOCOLATE CHIP COOKIES

ORIGINATION DATE: 1993   JOB NO. DT52289443-CCC

DRAKE'S
DEVIL DOGS

☆   ♥   ☎   ✎   ✈   ✉   ✂   ☛   ✿

Here's a clone recipe for a favorite east coast treat that could even fool Rosie O'Donnell. The snack food–loving talk show hostess professes her love for these tasty Drake's goodies all the time on her daytime show. And who could blame her? It's hard not to relish the smooth, fluffy filling sandwiched between two tender devil's food cake fingers. I'll take a Devil Dog over a Twinkie any day of the week. For this clone recipe, we'll make the cakes from scratch. This will help us to create a flavor and texture closest to the original. But if you're feeling especially lazy, you can certainly use a devil's food cake mix in place of the scratch recipe here. Just make the filling with the recipe below and assemble your cakes the same way.

CAKE
1 egg
½ cup shortening
1¼ cups granulated sugar
1 cup milk
1 teaspoon vanilla
2⅓ cups all-purpose flour
½ cup cocoa
½ teaspoon salt
½ teaspoon baking powder

FILLING
2 cups marshmallow creme
   (1 7-ounce jar)
1 cup shortening
½ cup powdered sugar
½ teaspoon vanilla
⅛ teaspoon salt
2 teaspoons very hot water

1. Preheat oven to 400 degrees.
2. In a medium bowl, blend together the egg, shortening, and

sugar with an electric mixer. Continue beating while adding the milk and vanilla.

3. In another bowl sift together remaining cake ingredients— flour, cocoa, salt, and baking powder.

4. Combine the dry ingredients with the wet ingredients and beat until smooth.

5. Spoon about a tablespoon of the batter in strips about 4 inches long and 1 inch wide on a lightly greased cookie sheet. Bake for 5 to 6 minutes or until the cakes are done. Cool.

6. In another bowl combine the marshmallow creme, shortening, powdered sugar, and vanilla. Dissolve the 1/8 teaspoon of salt in the 2 teaspoons of very hot water in a small bowl. Add this salt solution to the filling mixture and beat on high speed with an electric mixer until the filling is smooth and fluffy.

7. When the cakes have cooled, spread about a tablespoon of filling on the face of one cake and top it off with another cake. Repeat with the remaining ingredients.

• MAKES 20 TO 24 SNACK CAKES.

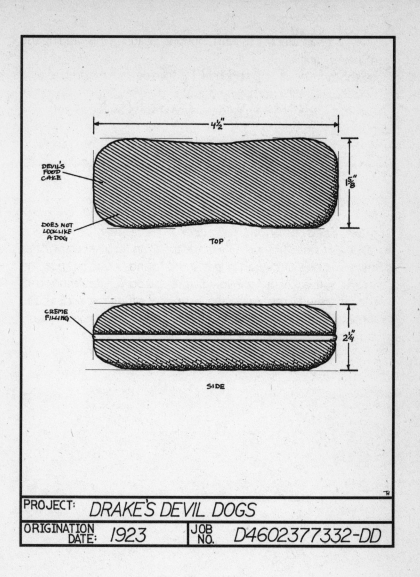

4½"

DEVIL'S
FOOD
CAKE

DOES NOT
LOOK LIKE
A DOG

1 5/8"

TOP

CREME
FILLING

2 1/4"

SIDE

TW

PROJECT: DRAKE'S DEVIL DOGS

ORIGINATION
DATE: 1923

JOB
NO. D4602377332-DD

EMERIL'S
ORIGINAL ESSENCE

☆　♥　☎　✎　✈　✉　✂　☞　✿

On his Food Network TV show Emeril Lagasse mentions "Essence" almost as much as "Bam!" and "Kick it up a notch!" He claims to put his special spice blend on "everything but ice cream." He suggests using it on all your meats, veggies, and pasta, and combining it with oil to use as a marinade. If you can't get your hands on the real thing, here's how to whip up a quick clone at home.

4 teaspoons popcorn salt (fine salt)

2 teaspoons paprika

1 teaspoon ground black pepper

½ teaspoon Schilling poultry seasoning

½ teaspoon cayenne pepper

½ teaspoon garlic powder

½ teaspoon onion powder

½ teaspoon dried thyme

½ teaspoon dried oregano

Combine all ingredients in a small bowl. Store in a covered container.

• MAKES ¼ CUP.

FATBURGER
ORIGINAL BURGER

☆　♥　☎　✎　✈　✉　✂　☞　❀

Southern California—the birthplace of famous hamburgers from McDonald's to Carl's Jr. and In-n-Out Burger—is home to another thriving burger chain that opened its first outlet in 1952. Lovie Yancey thought of the perfect name for the ⅓-pound burgers she sold at her Los Angeles burger joint: Fatburger. Now with over 41 units in California, Nevada, and moving into Washington and Arizona, Fatburger has become the food critics' favorite, winning "best burger in town" honors with regularity. The secret is the seasoned salt used on a big 'ol lean beef patty. And there's no ketchup on the stock version, just mayo, mustard, and relish. Replace the ground beef with ground turkey and you've got Fatburger's Turkeyburger all up and cloned.

⅓ pound lean ground beef
seasoned salt
ground black pepper
1 plain hamburger bun
½ tablespoon mayonnaise
¼ cup chopped iceberg lettuce
1 tomato slice
½ tablespoon mustard

½ tablespoon sweet pickle relish
1 tablespoon chopped onion
3 dill pickle slices (hamburger
　slices)

OPTIONAL
1 slice American cheese

1. Form the ground beef into a patty that is about 1 inch wider than the circumference of the hamburger bun.
2. Preheat a non-stick frying pan to medium/high heat. Fry the patty in the pan for 3 to 4 minutes per side or until done.

Season both sides of the beef with seasoned salt and ground black pepper.

3. As the meat cooks prepare the bun by spreading approximately ½ tablespoon of mayonnaise on the face of the top bun.
4. Place the lettuce on the mayonnaise, followed by the tomato slice.
5. When the beef is done place the patty on the bottom bun.
6. Spread about ½ tablespoon of mustard over the top of the beef patty.
7. Spoon about ½ tablespoon of relish over the mustard.
8. Sprinkle the chopped onion onto the relish.
9. Arrange the pickles on the chopped onion.
10. Bring the two halves of the burger together and serve with gumption.

- MAKES 1 BURGER.

TIDBITS

If you want cheese on your burger, put a slice of American cheese on the face of the bottom bun before adding the beef patty. The heat from the meat will melt the cheese.

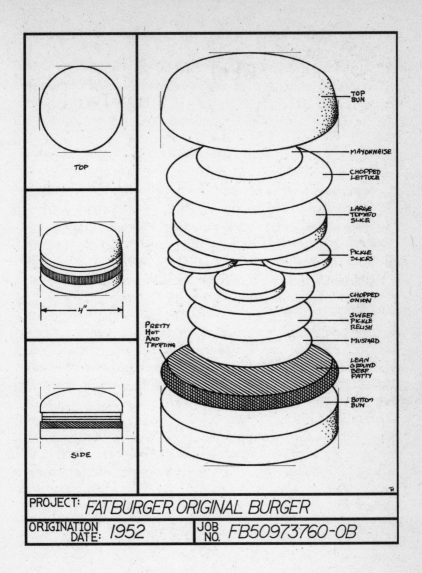

TOP

4"

SIDE

TOP BUN

MAYONNAISE

CHOPPED LETTUCE

LARGE TOMATO SLICE

PICKLE SLICES

CHOPPED ONION

SWEET PICKLE RELISH

MUSTARD

LEAN GROUND BEEF PATTY

BOTTOM BUN

PRETTY HOT AND TEMPTING

PROJECT: *FATBURGER ORIGINAL BURGER*

ORIGINATION DATE: *1952*

JOB NO. *FB50973760-OB*

FRENCH'S
CLASSIC YELLOW MUSTARD

☆　♥　☎　✎　✈　✉　✂　☛　✿

Americans' passion for yellow mustard began in St. Louis at the 1904 World's Fair when the tangy sauce was spread over the top of the classic American hot dog. Today, nearly 100 years later, French's mustard is the top brand found in restaurants, and 80 percent of U.S. households have a bottle of French's somewhere in the pantry or fridge. Another statistic shows that exactly one hundred percent of those bottles will ooze clear, runny mustard goo on the first squirt. And all those bottles will eventually run dry. If that happens just before you throw together some tasty dogs or drippy sandwiches, you may need to whip up some of your own yellow mustard to come to the rescue. If you've got dry ground mustard and turmeric on the spice rack, you can easily clone some yellow mustard sauce in no time at all. This recipe yields just ¼ cup of yellow mustard, but that should hold you over. At least until you can get to the market for more of the real thing.

4 teaspoons dry ground mustard
¼ cup water
3 tablespoons white distilled
　vinegar
½ teaspoon Wondra flour

¼ teaspoon plus ⅛ teaspoon salt
⅛ teaspoon turmeric
pinch garlic powder
pinch paprika

1. Combine all ingredients in a small saucepan over medium heat. Whisk until smooth.

2. When the mixture comes to a boil, reduce heat and simmer for 5 minutes, stirring often.
3. Remove the pan from the heat and cover until cool. Chill in a covered container.

- MAKES ¼ CUP.

GIRL SCOUT COOKIES
SHORTBREAD

☆ ♥ ☎ ✎ ✈ ✉ ✂ ☞ ✿

Since they only sell these once a year, right around springtime, you're bound to crave them again sometime in the fall. If you're still holding on to a box, by that time they may have begun to taste a bit like used air-hockey pucks. Now you can toss out those relics and fill the box with a fresh batch, made from this clone recipe for the first variety of cookies sold by the Girl Scouts back in 1917.

½ cup butter-flavored shortening
1 cup powdered sugar
½ teaspoon vanilla
¼ teaspoon salt
2 tablespoons beaten egg
½ teaspoon baking soda

2 tablespoons buttermilk
1 ½ cups all-purpose flour (plus an extra ¼ cup reserved for rolling)
⅛ teaspoon baking powder

1. In a large mixing bowl, cream together the shortening, sugar, vanilla, and salt with an electric mixer.
2. Add the egg and beat mixture until it's fluffy. Add the baking soda and mix for about 20 seconds, then add the buttermilk and mix for an additional 30 seconds.
3. In another bowl, combine the flour and baking powder.
4. Pour dry ingredients into wet ingredients and mix well with an electric mixer until flour is incorporated.
5. Roll the dough into a ball, cover it with plastic wrap, and chill it for 1 hour.
6. Preheat oven to 325 degrees.

7. Roll dough out on a well-floured surface to ⅛ inch thick and punch out cookies with a 1½ to 2-inch cutter (a medium-size spice bottle lid works well). Arrange cookies on an ungreased cookie sheet.

8. Bake for 12 to 15 minutes or until golden brown.

• MAKES 60 COOKIES.

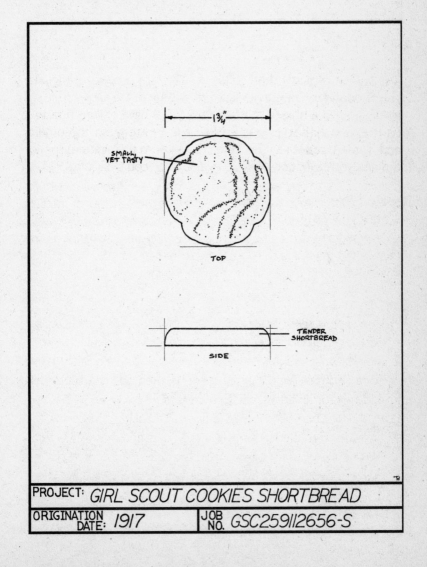

SMALL, YET TASTY

1¾"

TOP

TENDER SHORTBREAD

SIDE

PROJECT: *GIRL SCOUT COOKIES SHORTBREAD*

ORIGINATION DATE: *1917*   JOB NO. *GSC259112656-S*

GIRL SCOUT COOKIES
THIN MINTS

☆　♥　☎　✐　✈　▣　✂　☞　✿

If those cute little cookie peddlers aren't posted outside the market, it may be tough to get your hands on these—the most popular cookies sold by the Girl Scouts each year. One out of every four boxes of cookies sold by the girls is Thin Mints. This recipe uses an improved version of the chocolate wafers created for the Oreo cookie clone in the second *TSR* book, *More Top Secret Recipes*. That recipe creates 108 cookie wafers, so when you're done dipping, you'll have the equivalent of three boxes of the Girl Scout Cookies favorite. (See? That's why you bought those extra cookie sheets.) You could, of course, reduce the recipe by baking only ⅓ of the cookie dough for the wafers and then reducing the coating ingredients by ⅓, giving you a total of 36 cookies.

CHOCOLATE COOKIE WAFERS

1 18.25-ounce package Betty Crocker chocolate fudge cake mix
3 tablespoons shortening, melted
½ cup cake flour, measured then sifted
1 egg
3 tablespoons water
non-stick cooking spray

COATING

3 12-ounce bags semi-sweet chocolate chips
¾ teaspoon peppermint extract
6 tablespoons shortening

1. Combine the cookie ingredients in a large bowl, adding the water a little bit at a time until the dough forms. Cover and chill for 2 hours.

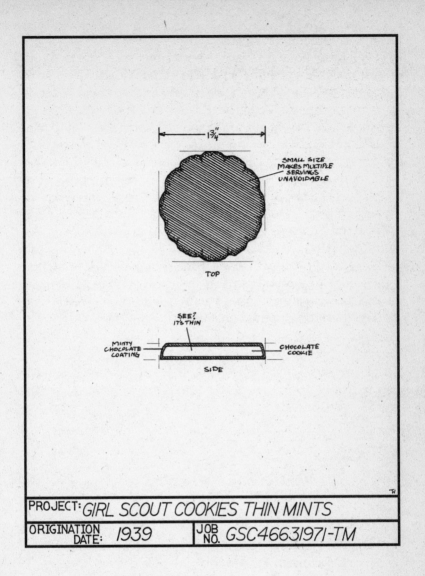

1¾"

SMALL SIZE
MAKES MULTIPLE
SERVINGS
UNAVOIDABLE

TOP

SEE?
IT'S THIN

MINTY
CHOCOLATE
COATING

CHOCOLATE
COOKIE

SIDE

PROJECT: *GIRL SCOUT COOKIES THIN MINTS*

ORIGINATION
DATE: *1939*

JOB
NO. *GSC4663I97I-TM*

65

2. Preheat oven to 350 degrees.
3. On a lightly floured surface roll out a portion of the dough to just under $\frac{1}{16}$ of an inch thick. To cut, use a lid from a spice container with a 1½-inch diameter (Schilling brand is good). Arrange the cut dough rounds on a cookie sheet that is sprayed with a light coating of non-stick spray. Bake for 10 minutes. Remove wafers from the oven and cool completely.
4. Combine chocolate chips with peppermint extract and shortening in a large microwave-safe glass or ceramic bowl. Heat on 50 percent power for 2 minutes, stir gently, then heat for an additional minute. Stir once again, and if chocolate is not a smooth consistency, continue to zap in microwave in 30-second intervals until smooth.
5. Use a fork to dip each wafer in the chocolate, tap the fork on the edge of the bowl so that the excess chocolate runs off, and then place the cookies side-by-side on a wax paper–lined baking sheet. Refrigerate until firm.

• MAKES 108 COOKIES.

GOOD SEASONS
ITALIAN SALAD DRESSING MIX

☆ ♥ ☎ ✎ ✈ ✉ ✂ ☞ ✿

Here's a clone for the instant dressing mix you buy in the little .7-ounce packets. When added to vinegar, water, and oil, you get one of the best-tasting instant salad dressings around. But what if you can't find the stuff, or it's no longer sold in your area, as I've heard from so many? Or maybe you want to save some money by making a bunch of your own? Just use the recipe below to make as much dry mix as you want, and save it for when you need instant salad satisfaction. I've used McCormick lemon pepper in the recipe here because it contains lemon juice solids that help duplicate the taste of the sodium citrate and citric acid in the real thing. The dry pectin, which can be found near the canning supplies in your supermarket, is used as a thickener, much like the xanthan gum in the original product.

1 teaspoon carrot, grated and
    finely chopped
1 teaspoon red bell pepper, finely
    minced
¾ teaspoon McCormick lemon
    pepper
⅛ teaspoon dried parsley flakes

1 teaspoon salt
¼ teaspoon garlic powder
⅛ teaspoon onion powder
2 teaspoons sugar
⅛ teaspoon black pepper
2 teaspoons dry pectin
pinch ground oregano

1. Place the carrot and bell pepper on a baking pan in an oven set on 250 degrees for 45 to 60 minutes, or until all of the small pieces are completely dry, but not browned.
2. Combine the dried carrot and bell pepper with the other

ingredients in a small bowl. Mix can be stored in a sealed container indefinitely until needed.

3. When ready to use, pour ¼ cup of vinegar into a cruet or jar. Add 3 tablespoons of water, then the dressing mix. Seal and shake vigorously. Add ½ cup of oil and shake until well blended.

• SERVES 8 TO 10.

TIDBITS

If you would like to make the dressing with less oil, follow step 3 above as directed, but substitute ¼ cup of water and ¼ cup of oil in place of the ½ cup of oil.

GRANDMA'S COOKIES
OATMEAL RAISIN BIG COOKIES

☆ ♥ ☏ ✎ ✈ ✉ ✄ ☛ ✿

GrandMa's Cookie Company was founded back in 1914 by Foster Wheeler, but it wasn't until 1977 that the company introduced the popular Big Cookie. This large, soft cookie comes two to a pack and is offered in several varieties, including oatmeal raisin. Now you can bake up a couple batches all your own with this spiffy kitchen clone. Just be sure not to overdo it in the oven. You want these cookies soft and chewy when cool—just like a happy grandma would make 'em. So be sure to take the cookies out when they are just beginning to turn light brown around the edges.

½ cup raisins
⅓ cup water
½ cup vegetable shortening
1 egg
1½ cups dark brown sugar
1½ teaspoons vanilla

2 cups all-purpose flour
1¼ cups oats (not instant)
2 teaspoons baking soda
¾ teaspoon cinnamon
1 teaspoon salt
½ cup raisins

1. Preheat oven to 275 degrees.
2. Combine ½ cup raisins with water in a food processor and blend on high speed for about 1 minute or until very smooth.
3. Combine this raisin puree with the vegetable shortening, egg, brown sugar, and vanilla in a large bowl. Mix well with electric mixer until smooth.
4. In a separate bowl, combine the flour with the oats, baking soda, cinnamon, and salt. Pour this dry mixture into the wet

mixture and mix well until ingredients are incorporated. Mix in ½ cup raisins.

5. Roll 3-tablespoon-size portions of the dough into a ball in your hands and press to ½ inch flat on an ungreased baking sheet. Bake for 18 to 20 minutes. Be careful not to overcook, or the cookies will not be chewy. Store in a sealed container.

• MAKES 16 TO 18 COOKIES.

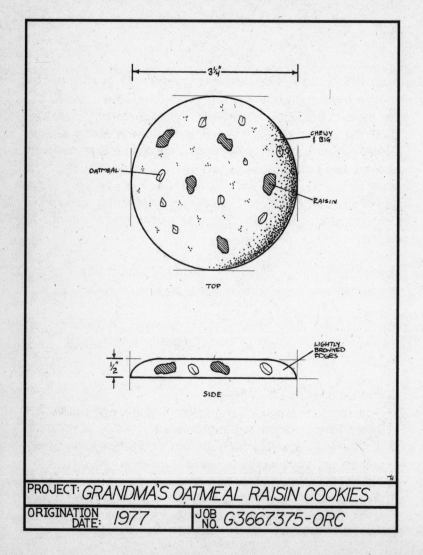

PROJECT: GRANDMA'S OATMEAL RAISIN COOKIES

ORIGINATION DATE: 1977   JOB NO. G3667375-ORC

GRANDMA'S COOKIES
PEANUT BUTTER
BIG COOKIES

☆　♥　☎　✎　✈　✉　✂　☛　✿

When these cookies are cool, be sure to seal them up real super duper tight in something like Tupperware or a Ziploc bag. That's the way to keep these puppies moist and chewy like the original GrandMa's Big Cookies. In fact, the real product claims to be the only national cookie brand that guarantees the freshness of the product or double your money back. That's very big of the current manufacturer, Frito-Lay, which purchased the GrandMa's Cookies brand from General Mills back in 1980.

½ cup vegetable shortening
½ cup Peter Pan peanut butter
  (smooth, not chunky)
1¼ cups packed dark brown
  sugar

1 egg
1 teaspoon vanilla
¾ teaspoon salt
1½ cups all-purpose flour
2 teaspoons baking soda

1. Preheat oven to 275 degrees.
2. Beat shortening, peanut butter, brown sugar, egg, vanilla, and salt together in large bowl until smooth.
3. In a separate bowl combine the flour and baking soda. Slowly add the dry mixture to the wet mixture while beating.
4. Roll 3-tablespoon-size portions of the dough into a ball in your hands and press to ½ inch flat on an ungreased baking sheet. Bake for 18 to 20 minutes. Be careful not to overcook,

or the cookies will not be chewy, negatively impacting the full
enjoyment potential of the product.

- MAKES 14 TO 16 COOKIES.

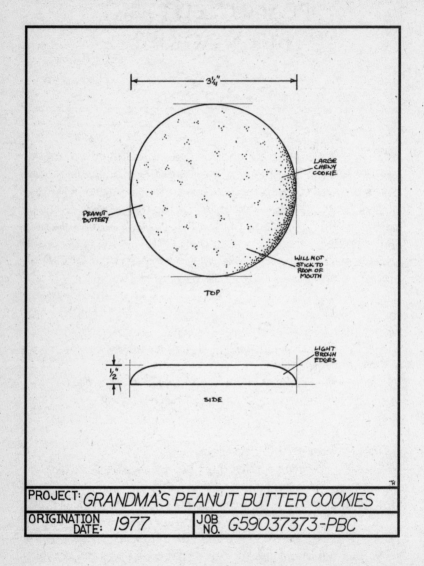

GREAT AMERICAN COOKIES SNICKERDOODLES

☆　♥　☎　✎　✈　✉　✂　☛　✿

Rather than trying to beat the competitors—especially if they have an exceptional product—Mrs. Fields Famous Brands waves the cash at 'em. With the acquisition of Great American Cookies in 1998 by the company that made chewy mall cookies big business, Mrs. Fields is now peddling her baked wares in more than 90 percent of the premier shopping malls in the United States. That's how you make the dough! One of the all-time favorites you can snag at any of the 364 Great American Cookies outlets is the classic snickerdoodle. Rolled in cinnamon and sugar, it's soft and chewy like the other cookies, and will seem to be undercooked when you take it out of the oven. When it cools it should be gooey, yet firm in the middle. Just a couple bites should make you wonder: "Got milk?!"

½ cup butter (1 stick), softened
½ cup granulated sugar
⅓ cup brown sugar
1 egg
½ teaspoon vanilla
1 ½ cups flour
¼ teaspoon salt

½ teaspoon baking soda
¼ teaspoon cream of tartar

TOPPING
2 tablespoons granulated sugar
1 teaspoon cinnamon

1. In a large bowl, cream together the butter and sugars with an electric mixer on high speed. Add the egg and vanilla and beat until smooth.

2. In another bowl, combine the flour, salt, baking soda, and cream of tartar.
3. Pour the dry ingredients into the wet ingredients and mix well.
4. Let the dough rest for 30 to 60 minutes in the refrigerator. Preheat oven to 300 degrees.
5. In a small bowl, combine the sugar with the cinnamon for the topping.
6. Take about 2½ tablespoons of the dough and roll it into a ball. Roll this dough in the cinnamon/sugar mixture and press it onto an ungreased cookie sheet. Repeat for the remaining cookies.
7. Bake the cookies for 12 to 14 minutes and no more. The cookies may seem undercooked, but will continue to develop after they are removed from the oven. When the cookies have cooled they should be soft and chewy in the middle.

• MAKES 16 TO 18 COOKIES.

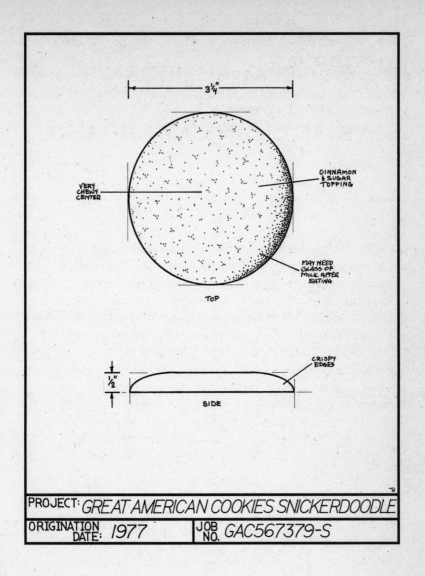

3¼"

VERY CHEWY CENTER

CINNAMON & SUGAR TOPPING

MAY NEED GLASS OF MILK AFTER EATING

TOP

½"

CRISPY EDGES

SIDE

PROJECT: GREAT AMERICAN COOKIES SNICKERDOODLE

ORIGINATION DATE: 1977

JOB NO. GAC567379-S

GREAT AMERICAN COOKIES
WHITE CHUNK MACADAMIA

☆　♥　☎　✎　✈　✉　✂　☛　✿

When Arthur Karp shared his grandmother's favorite chocolate chip cookie recipe with Michael Coles, the business partners knew they had a hit on their hands. They opened their first Great American Cookies store in 1977 in The Perimeter Mall in Atlanta, Georgia. Now with more than 350 stores in the chain, these cookies have quickly become a favorite, just begging to be cloned. The chain bakes the cookies in convection ovens at the low temperature of 280 degrees for around 16 to 17 minutes. But since most of us don't have convection ovens and may have a hard time getting the oven temperature to this odd setting, I've made some adjustments. Just be sure, when you remove the cookies from the oven, that they appear undercooked and light brown around the edges. This will give the cookies the perfect chewy texture when cool.

½ cup butter (1 stick), softened
1 cup brown sugar
½ cup coconut flakes, finely minced
1 egg
1 tablespoon milk
1 teaspoon vanilla

1½ cups flour
2 teaspoons baking soda
½ teaspoon baking powder
½ teaspoon salt
8 ounces solid white chocolate, cut into chunks
1 cup macadamia nuts, chopped

1. Cream together the butter and sugar in a large bowl with a mixer on high speed.

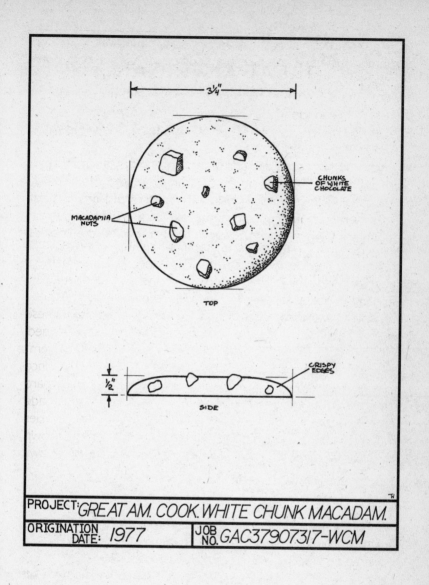

TOP

SIDE

3¼"

CHUNKS
OF WHITE
CHOCOLATE

MACADAMIA
NUTS

½"

CRISPY
EDGES

PROJECT: *GREAT AM. COOK. WHITE CHUNK MACADAM.*

ORIGINATION
DATE: *1977*

JOB
NO. *GAC37907317-WCM*

2. Add the coconut, egg, milk, and vanilla and mix well.
3. In another bowl combine the flour, baking soda, baking powder, and salt.
4. Add the dry mixture to the wet mixture and mix until dough forms. Mix in the white chocolate and macadamia nuts.
5. Let the dough rest for 30 to 60 minutes in the refrigerator. Preheat oven to 300 degrees.
6. Measure out about 2½ tablespoons of the dough and form a ball. Drop each ball of dough onto an ungreased cookie sheet about 3 inches apart and bake for 12 to 14 minutes. Do not overbake! Cookies should come out of the oven appearing slightly browned, yet undercooked. When cooled the cookies will be soft and chewy like the original.

• MAKES 16 TO 18 COOKIES.

HEINZ
57 SAUCE

☆　♥　☎　✎　✈　✉　✂　☞　❀

In the late 1800s Henry John Heinz established the slogan "57 Varieties," which you can still find printed on Heinz products even though the company now boasts over 5700 varieties in 200 countries. Today Heinz is the world's largest tomato-product producer, but interestingly the first product for the company that was launched in 1869 had nothing to do with tomatoes; it was grated horseradish. It wasn't until 1876 that ketchup was added to the growing company's product line. Tomato is also an important ingredient in this tangy steak sauce. But you'll find some interesting ingredients in there as well, such as raisin puree, malt vinegar, apple juice concentrate, and mustard. And don't worry if your version doesn't come out as brown as the original. Heinz uses a little caramel coloring in its product to give it that distinctive tint. It's just for looks, though, so I've left that ingredient out of this clone recipe. Besides, I've found that the turmeric and yellow mustard will still help get this version pretty close to the color of the real deal.

RAISIN PUREE
½ cup raisins
½ cup water

1⅓ cups white vinegar
1 cup tomato paste
⅔ cup malt vinegar
⅔ cup sugar

½ cup water
1 tablespoon yellow prepared
   mustard
2 teaspoons apple juice concentrate
1½ teaspoons salt
1 teaspoon vegetable oil
1 teaspoon lemon juice

½ teaspoon onion powder
¼ teaspoon garlic powder
⅛ teaspoon turmeric

1. Make the raisin puree by combining the raisins with the water in a food processor or blender. Blend on high speed for 1 minute or until the puree is smooth. Measure ¼ cup of this puree into a medium saucepan.
2. Add the remaining ingredients and whisk until smooth.
3. Turn heat up to medium high and bring mixture to a thorough boil. Reduce heat to low and simmer, uncovered, for ½ hour or until thick. Let sauce cool and then refrigerate it in a covered container for at least 24 hours.

• MAKES 3 CUPS.

HEINZ
KETCHUP

☆　♥　☎　✎　✈　✉　✂　☞　✿

By the age of 12 Henry John Heinz was peddling produce from his family's garden in post–Civil War Pittsburgh. By age 25, he and a friend had launched Heinz & Noble to sell bottled horseradish in clear glass bottles to reveal its purity. Henry's pickling empire grew as he added jams, jellies, and condiments to the line, including ketchup, which hit the markets in 1876. You'll still see the famous Heinz pickle logo on every product, and if you want a quick tip on how to get the thick stuff out of the bottle easily, don't pound on the backside like a maniac. Instead Heinz recommends a good smack to the embossed "57" found on the neck of every bottle. Today Heinz is the world's largest tomato processor, with the famous ketchup bottles in over half of U.S. households. But if you find your house is all out, just create a simple clone with a few common ingredients. You'll get a whole 12-ounce bottle's worth of thick, tasty ketchup with this one-of-a-kind secret recipe.

One 6-ounce can tomato
　paste
½ cup light corn syrup
½ cup white vinegar
¼ cup water

1 tablespoon sugar
1 teaspoon salt
¼ teaspoon onion
　powder
⅛ teaspoon garlic powder

1. Combine all ingredients in a medium saucepan over medium heat. Whisk until smooth.

2. When mixture comes to a boil, reduce heat and simmer for 20 minutes, stirring often.
4. Remove pan from heat and cover until cool. Chill in a covered container.

- MAKES 1 ½ CUPS.

HERSHEY'S
PAYDAY CANDY BAR

☆ ♥ ☎ ✎ ✈ ✉ ✂ ☞ ✿

In December of 1996, Hershey Foods snagged the U.S. operations of Leaf Brands for a pretty penny. This added several well-known candies to Hershey's already impressive roster, including Good & Plenty, Jolly Rancher, Milk Duds, Whoppers, Heath, and this delicious peanut roll, which we can now clone at home. The center is sort of a white fudge that we can make by combining a few ingredients on the stove, then getting the mixture up to just the right temperature using a candy thermometer (you've got one, right?). Once cool, this candy center is coated with a thin layer of caramel, then quickly pressed onto roasted peanuts. Looks just like the real thing! This recipe will make eight candy bars. But it's up to you to make the dental appointment.

CENTERS

¼ cup whole milk
5 unwrapped caramels
1 tablespoon light corn syrup
1 teaspoon smooth peanut butter
¼ teaspoon vanilla

¼ teaspoon salt
1¼ cups powdered sugar
20 unwrapped caramels
1½ teaspoons water
2 cups dry roasted peanuts

1. Combine all ingredients for the centers, except the powdered sugar, in a small saucepan over low heat. Stir often as the caramel slowly melts. When the mixture is smooth, add ¾ cup of powdered sugar. Stir. Save the remaining ½ cup of powdered sugar for later.

2. Use a candy thermometer to bring the mixture to exactly 230 degrees, stirring often, then turn off the heat.

3. When the temperature of the candy begins to drop, add the remaining ½ cup powdered sugar to the pan, then use a hand mixer on high speed to combine. Keep mixing until the candy cools and thickens and can no longer be mixed. That should take a minute or two.

4. Let the candy cool in the pan for 10 to 15 minutes, or until it can be touched. Don't let it sit too long—you want the candy to still be warm and pliable when you shape it. Take a tablespoon-size portion and roll it between your palms or on a countertop until it forms a roll the width of your index finger and measures about 4½ inches long. Repeat with the remaining center candy mixture and place the rolls on wax paper. You should have 8 rolls. Let the center rolls sit out for an hour or two to firm up.

5. Combine the 20 caramels with the 1½ teaspoons of water in a small saucepan over low heat. Stir often until the caramels melt completely, then turn off the heat. If you work fast this caramel will stay warm while you make the candy bars.

6. Pour the peanuts onto a baking sheet or other flat surface. Using a basting brush and working quickly, "paint" a coating of caramel onto one side of a center roll. Quickly turn the center over, caramel-side-down, onto the peanuts and press gently so that the peanuts stick to the surface of the candy. Paint more caramel onto the other side of the roll and press it down onto the peanuts. The candy should have a solid layer of peanuts covering all sides. If needed, brush additional caramel onto the roll, then turn it onto the peanuts to coat the roll completely. Place the candy bar onto wax paper, and repeat with the remaining ingredients. Eat when completely cool.

• MAKES 8 CANDY BARS.

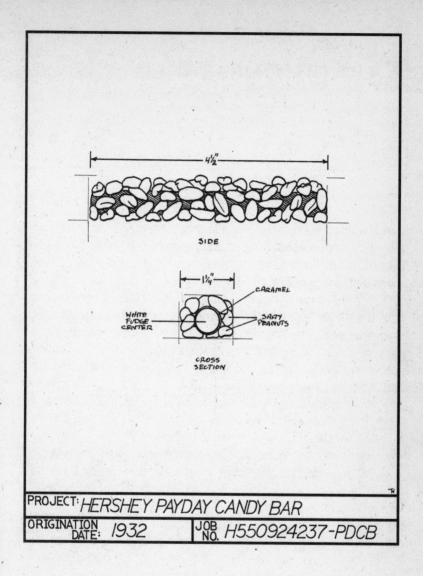

4½"

SIDE

1¼"

CARAMEL

WHITE
FUDGE
CENTER

SALTY
PEANUTS

CROSS
SECTION

PROJECT: *HERSHEY PAYDAY CANDY BAR*	
ORIGINATION DATE: *1932*	JOB NO. *H550924237-PDCB*

HONEYBAKED
HAM GLAZE

☆　♥　☎　✎　✈　✉　✂　☞　✿

TSR has discovered that the tender hams are delivered to each of the 300 HoneyBaked outlets already smoked, but without the glaze. It is only when the ham gets to your local HoneyBaked store that a special machine thin-slices the tender meat in a spiral fashion around the bone. One at a time, each ham is then coated with the glaze—a blend that is similar to what might be used to make pumpkin pie. This sweet coating is then caramelized with a blowtorch by hand until the glaze bubbles and melts, turning golden brown. If needed, more of the coating is added, and the blowtorch is fired up until the glaze is just right. It's this careful process that turns the same size ham that costs 10 dollars in a supermarket into one that customers gladly shell out 3 to 4 times as much to share during the holiday season.

For this clone recipe, we will re-create the glaze that you can apply to a smoked/cooked bone-in ham of your choice. Look for a ham that's presliced. Otherwise you'll have to slice it yourself with a sharp knife, then the glaze will be applied. To get the coating just right you must use a blowtorch. If you don't have one, you can find a small one in hardware stores for around 10 to 15 bucks. And don't worry—I didn't leave out an ingredient. No honey is necessary to re-create this favorite holiday glaze.

1 fully cooked shank half ham,
   bone-in (presliced)
1 cup sugar
1/4 teaspoon ground cinnamon
1/4 teaspoon ground nutmeg

1/4 teaspoon ground clove
1/8 teaspoon paprika
dash ground ginger
dash ground allspice

1. If you couldn't find a presliced ham, the first thing you must do is slice it. Use a very sharp knife to cut the ham into very thin slices around the bone. Do not cut all the way down to the bone or the meat may not hold together properly as it is being glazed. You want the slices to be quite thin, but not so thin that they begin to fall apart or off the bone. You may wish to turn the ham onto its flat end and cut around it starting at the bottom. You can then spin the ham as you slice around and work your way up.
2. Mix the remaining ingredients together in a small bowl.
3. Lay down a couple sheets of wax paper onto a flat surface, such as your kitchen counter. Pour the sugar mixture onto the wax paper and spread it around evenly.
4. Pick up the ham and roll it over the sugar mixture so that it is well coated. Do not coat the flat end of the ham, just the outer, presliced surface.
5. Turn the ham onto its flat end on a plate. Use a blowtorch with a medium-size flame to caramelize the sugar. Wave the torch over the sugar with rapid movement, so that the sugar bubbles and browns, but does not burn. Spin the plate so that you can torch the entire surface of the ham. Repeat the coating and caramelizing process until the ham has been well glazed (don't expect to use all of the sugar mixture). Serve the ham cold or reheated, just like the real thing.

• MAKES 1 HOLIDAY HAM.

HOT DOG
ON A STICK
HOT DOG

☆　　♥　　☎　　✎　　✈　　✉　　✂　　☞　　✿

One hot summer day in 1946 Dave Barham was inspired to dip a hot dog into his mother's cornbread batter, then deep fry it to a golden brown. Dave soon found a quaint Santa Monica, California, location near the beach to sell his new creation with mustard on the side and a tall glass of ice-cold lemonade. Be sure you find the shorter dogs, not "bun-length." In this case size does matter. Snag some of the disposable wood chopsticks from a local Chinese or Japanese restaurant next time you're there and start dipping.

8 to 10 cups vegetable oil	1 teaspoon baking soda
2 cups flour	1¾ cups fat-free milk
¾ cup cornmeal	2 egg yolks, slightly beaten
½ cup sugar	8 to 10 turkey hot dogs
1¾ teaspoons salt	5 pairs chopsticks

1. Preheat oil in a deep pan or fryer to 375 degrees.
2. Combine the flour, cornmeal, sugar, salt, and baking soda in a large bowl.
3. Add the milk and egg yolks to the dry ingredients and mix with an electric mixer on high speed until batter is smooth.
4. Dry off the hot dogs with a paper towel. Jab the thin end of a single chopstick about halfway into the end of each hot dog.
5. When the oil is hot, tip the bowl of batter so that you can completely coat each hot dog. Roll the hot dog in the batter until it is entirely covered.
6. Hold the hot dog up by the stick and let some of the bat-

ter drip off. Quickly submerge the hot dog in the oil and spin it slowly so that the coating cooks evenly. After about 20 seconds you can use a lid to the deep fryer or pan to put weight on the stick, keeping the hot dog fully immersed in the oil. You can cook a couple dogs at a time this way. Cook for 5 to 6 minutes or until coating is dark brown. Turn them once or twice as they cook. Drain on paper towels while cooling, and repeat with the remaining hot dogs.

- MAKES 8 TO 10 HOT DOGS.

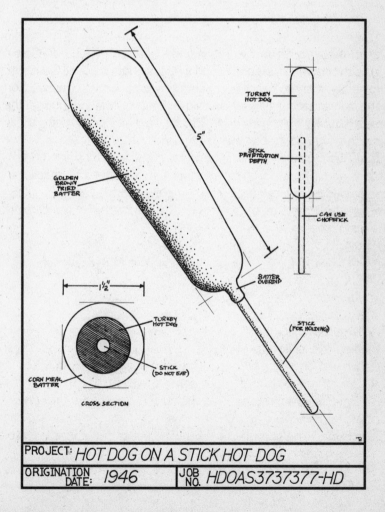

TURKEY HOT DOG

STICK PENETRATION DEPTH

CAN USE CHOPSTICK

GOLDEN BROWN FRIED BATTER

5"

BATTER OVERDIP

1½"

TURKEY HOT DOG

STICK (FOR HOLDING)

STICK (DO NOT EAT)

CORN MEAL BATTER

CROSS SECTION

PROJECT:	*HOT DOG ON A STICK HOT DOG*
ORIGINATION DATE: *1946*	JOB NO. *HDOAS3737377-HD*

K.C. MASTERPIECE
ORIGINAL BBQ SAUCE

☆　♥　☎　✎　✈　✉　✂　☞　✿

Even though it's now owned and produced by the Clorox Company, the taste of Original K.C. Masterpiece barbecue sauce is the same as when it was first created in good ol' Kansas City, USA. This is the sauce that steals awards from all the other popular meat slathers on the market. Now it's sold in a variety of flavors. But this is the clone for the original, and you'll find it very easy to make. Just throw all of the ingredients in a saucepan, crank it up to a boil, and simmer for about an hour. Done deal. And just like the original Masterpiece, this stuff will make a work of art out of any of your grilled meats, or burgers and sandwiches, and as a dipping sauce or marinade.

2 cups water
¾ cup light corn syrup
½ cup tomato paste
½ cup vinegar
3 tablespoons molasses
3 tablespoons brown sugar

1 teaspoon liquid smoke (see Tidbit)
½ teaspoon salt
¼ teaspoon onion powder
¼ teaspoon pepper
⅛ teaspoon paprika
⅛ teaspoon garlic powder

1. Combine all ingredients in a medium saucepan over high heat and whisk until smooth.
2. Bring mixture to a boil, then reduce heat and simmer for 45 to 60 minutes or until mixture is thick.

3. Cool, then store in a covered container in the refrigerator overnight so that flavors can develop.

- MAKES 1½ CUPS.

TIDBITS

Liquid smoke is a flavoring found near the barbecue sauces and marinades. Use hickory-flavored liquid smoke if you have a choice.

KELLOGG'S
COCOA RICE KRISPIES TREATS

☆   ♥   ☎   ✎   ✈   ⊠   ✂   ☛   ✿

It's the Rice Krispies Treat for all you chocolate lovers. By simply replacing regular Rice Krispies with Kellogg's Cocoa Krispies, then adding a bit of cocoa to the recipe, we can clone the exact flavor of the product you otherwise have to buy in boxes in the grocery store. This recipe makes 16 of the crunchy brown bars, or the equivalent of two boxes of the real thing.

3 tablespoons margarine	4 teaspoons cocoa
¼ teaspoon salt	6 cups Cocoa Krispies cereal
5 cups miniature marshmallows	non-stick cooking spray
½ teaspoon vanilla	

1. Combine margarine and salt in a large saucepan over low heat.
2. When margarine has melted, add marshmallows and vanilla and stir until marshmallows have melted. Add cocoa and stir well. Remove from heat.
3. Add Cocoa Krispies and stir until the cereal is well coated with the melted marshmallow mixture.
4. Spray a 9 x 13-inch baking dish with a light coating of non-stick cooking spray. Pour the mixture into the dish and, using wax paper or lightly greased hands, press down until it's flat in the dish. Cool. Slice into 16 bars.

• MAKES 16 BARS.

KELLOGG'S PEANUT BUTTER CHOCOLATE RICE KRISPIES TREATS

☆   ♥   ☎   ✎   ✈   ✉   ✂   ☛   ✿

When Kellogg's reacted to spectacular sales of its Rice Krispies Treats with two new varieties of the popular and addictive snack, *TSR* got on the case. It seems we've all tasted the original Rice Krispies Treats. The homemade version is the second homework assignment in Cooking 101, after learning how to boil water. And the Kellogg's store-bought packaged version has been available to the lazier of us for several years now. This variety, however, puts that whole Reese's "You got your peanut butter in my chocolate" thing to work. The crunchy bar has just a touch of nutty essence that builds nicely on the other familiar flavors. But don't be fooled by that dark "chocolatey" coating on top of the real thing. It's not actually chocolate, but rather a melt-resistant custom blend of cocoa and ... uh, stuff, that tastes a lot like chocolate; and that happens to work better for the product from a manufacturing, shipping, and shelf-life aspect. But here in kitchen cloning land, we don't have to worry about those things. So get ready to walk on the wild side, people, as we step up to the microwave and melt some *real* chocolate chips for topping our cinch of a crunchy clone.

1 tablespoon margarine
3 tablespoons crunchy peanut
  butter
⅛ teaspoon salt
5 cups miniature marshmallows

½ teaspoon vanilla
6 cups Rice Krispies cereal
1 12-ounce bag milk chocolate
  chips
non-stick cooking spray

1. Combine margarine, peanut butter, and salt in a large saucepan over low heat.
2. When peanut butter and margarine have melted, add marshmallows and vanilla and stir until marshmallows have melted. Remove from heat.
3. Add Rice Krispies and stir until cereal is well coated with the melted marshmallow mixture.
4. Spray a 9 x 13-inch baking dish with a light coating of non-stick cooking spray. Pour the Rice Krispies mixture into the dish and, using wax paper or lightly greased hands, press down until it's flat in the dish. Cool.
5. Prepare the topping by pouring the chocolate chips into a glass dish. Microwave for 2 minutes on 50 percent power. Stir gently. Microwave for an additional minute on 50 percent power. Stir gently once more until smooth. If the mixture hasn't completely melted, zap it again for another 30 seconds.
6. Use a spatula to spread a thin layer of chocolate over the top of the Rice Krispies mixture. Cool at room temperature (at least 72 degrees), or chill until firm. Slice into 16 bars.

• MAKES 16 BARS.

KENNY ROGERS ROASTERS CORN MUFFINS

☆　♥　☎　✎　✈　✉　✂　☞　✿

He knows when to hold 'em, he knows when to fold 'em. And lately he's been folding 'em quite a bit as Kenny Rogers Roasters restaurants across the country have bolted their doors for lack of interest. Looks like that whole "home meal replacement" thing hasn't worked out too well for this fire-roasted–chicken chain. But that doesn't mean that Kenny didn't know how to make awesome corn muffins that are served with every meal. And since it's becoming harder and harder to find a Kenny Rogers Roasters outlet, we have no choice but to duplicate these at home if we want to re-create this part of the Kenny experience.

½ cup butter
⅔ cup sugar
¼ cup honey
2 eggs
½ teaspoon salt

1 ½ cups all-purpose flour
¾ cup yellow cornmeal
½ teaspoon baking powder
½ cup milk
¾ cup frozen yellow corn

1. Preheat oven to 400 degrees.
2. Cream together butter, sugar, honey, eggs, and salt in a large bowl.
3. Add flour, cornmeal, and baking powder and blend thoroughly. Add milk while mixing.
4. Add corn to mixture and combine by hand until corn is worked in.

5. Grease a 12-cup muffin pan and fill each cup with batter. Bake for 20 to 25 minutes or until muffins begin to turn brown on top.

• MAKES 12 MUFFINS.

KFC
BBQ BAKED BEANS

☆　　♥　　☎　　✐　　✈　　✉　　✄　　☛　　✿

Here's a clone recipe to add to the table for your next picnic, cookout, or all-purpose pig-out. Just find yourself a couple cans of the small white beans (be sure they're not pinto beans or great northern beans), and the rest is easy. Throw all of the ingredients into a casserole dish and let the sucker bake. While you get on with the party.

2 15-ounce cans small white
   beans (with liquid)
2 tablespoons water
1 tablespoon cornstarch
½ cup ketchup
½ cup dark brown sugar
2 tablespoons white vinegar

4 teaspoons minced fresh onion
2 pieces cooked bacon, crumbled
½ teaspoon dry mustard
¼ teaspoon salt
dash pepper
dash garlic powder

1. Preheat oven to 350 degrees.
2. Pour entire contents of two 15-ounce cans of beans into a covered casserole dish.
3. Combine the water with the cornstarch in a small bowl until cornstarch dissolves. Stir mixture into the beans.
4. Stir the remaining ingredients into the beans and cover the dish.
5. Bake for 90 minutes or until sauce thickens. Stir every 30 minutes. Let the beans sit for 5 to 10 minutes after removing them from the oven before serving.

• SERVES 4 TO 6.

KFC
EXTRA CRISPY CHICKEN

☆   ♥   ☎   ✎   ✈   ✉   ✂   ☞   ✿

In 1971, with KFC now out of his control, Colonel Harland Sanders was approached by the company's new owners, the Heublein Company, with a recipe for a crispier version of the famous fried chicken. The marketing department decided they wanted to call the product "Colonel Sanders' New Recipe" but the Colonel would have nothing to do with it. The stern and opinionated founder of the company, who had publicly criticized the changes to his secret formulas (in a newspaper interview he called the revised mashed potatoes "wallpaper paste"), refused to allow the use of his name on the product. Since the Colonel was an important component of the company's marketing plan, KFC appeased him. The new chicken was then appropriately dubbed "Extra Crispy," and sales were finger-licking good. Now you can reproduce the taste and crunchy breaded texture of the real thing with a marinating process similar to that used by the huge fast food chain, followed by a double-dipped coating. Unlike the Original Recipe chicken clone, which is pressure-cooked, this version is deep fried.

1 whole frying chicken, cut up
6 to 8 cups vegetable shortening

MARINADE
4 cups water
1 tablespoon salt
½ teaspoon MSG (see Tidbits)

COATING
1 egg, beaten
1 cup milk
2 cups all-purpose flour
2½ teaspoons salt
¾ teaspoon pepper
¾ teaspoon MSG (see Tidbits)

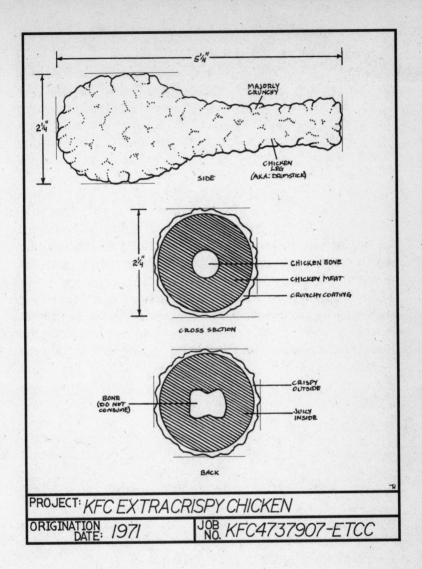

SIDE

5¼"

2¼"

MAJORLY
CRUNCHY

CHICKEN
LEG
(A.K.A.: DRUMSTICK)

2¼"

CHICKEN BONE

CHICKEN MEAT

CRUNCHY COATING

CROSS SECTION

BONE
(DO NOT
CONSUME)

CRISPY
OUTSIDE

JUICY
INSIDE

BACK

PROJECT: KFC EXTRA CRISPY CHICKEN

ORIGINATION DATE: 1971

JOB NO. KFC4737907-ETCC

1. Trim any excess skin and fat from the chicken pieces. Preheat the shortening in a deep fryer to 350 degrees.
2. Combine the water, salt, and ½ teaspoon MSG for the marinade in a large bowl. Add the chicken to the bowl and let it sit for 20 minutes. Turn the chicken a couple times as it marinates.
3. Combine the beaten egg and milk in a medium bowl. In another medium bowl, combine the remaining coating ingredients (flour, salt, pepper, and ¾ teaspoon MSG).
4. When the chicken has marinated, transfer each piece to paper towels so that excess liquid can drain off. Working with one piece at a time, first coat the chicken with the dry flour mixture, then the egg and milk mixture, and then back into the flour. Be sure that each piece is coated very generously. Stack the chicken on a plate or cookie sheet until each piece has been coated.
5. Drop the chicken, one piece at a time, into the hot shortening. Fry half of the chicken at a time (4 pieces) for 12 to 15 minutes, or until it is golden brown. You should be sure to stir the chicken around halfway through the cooking time so that each piece cooks evenly.
6. Remove the chicken to a rack to drain for about 5 minutes before eating.

- SERVES 3 TO 4 (8 PIECES OF CHICKEN).

TIDBITS

MSG is monosodium glutamate, the solid form of a natural amino acid found in many vegetables. It can be found in stores in the spice sections and as the brand name Accent Flavor Enhancer. MSG is an important component of several KFC items.

KFC
HONEY BBQ WINGS

☆   ♥   ☎   ✎   ✈   ✉   ✂   ☛   ✿

Once a regular menu item, these sweet, saucy wings are now added to the KFC menu on a "limited-time-only" basis in many markets. So how are we to get that sticky sauce all over our faces and hands during those months when we're cruelly denied our Honey BBQ Wings? Now it's as easy as whipping up a clone that re-creates a crispy breading on the chicken wings, and then slathering those puppies with a tasty knock-off of the sweet, tangy honey BBQ sauce. "Limited-time-only" signs—we laugh at you!

SAUCE

1¼ cups ketchup

⅓ cup white vinegar

¼ cup molasses

¼ cup honey

1 teaspoon liquid smoke
(see Tidbits)

½ teaspoon salt

¼ teaspoon onion powder

¼ teaspoon chili powder

6 to 8 cups vegetable shortening

1 egg, beaten

1 cup milk

2 cups all-purpose flour

2½ teaspoons salt

¾ teaspoon pepper

¾ teaspoon MSG (see Tidbits)

20 chicken wing pieces

1. Combine the sauce ingredients in a small saucepan over medium heat. Stir until ingredients are well combined and bring to a boil. Then reduce heat and simmer uncovered for 15 to 20 minutes.
2. As sauce is simmering, heat up 6 to 8 cups of shortening in a deep fryer set to 350 degrees.

3. Combine the beaten egg with the milk in a small bowl.
4. In another small bowl, combine the flour, salt, pepper, and MSG.
5. When the shortening is hot, dip each wing first in the flour mixture, then into the milk and egg mixture, and back into the flour. Arrange wings on a plate until each one is coated with batter.
6. Fry the wings for 9 to 12 minutes or until light golden brown. If you have a small fryer, you may wish to fry 10 of the wings at a time. Drain on a rack.
7. When the sauce is done, brush the entire surface of each wing with a light coating of sauce. Serve immediately.

- MAKES 2 TO 4 SERVINGS (20 WINGS).

TIDBITS

Liquid smoke is a flavoring found in the store near the barbecue sauces and marinades. Use hickory-flavored liquid smoke if you have a choice.

MSG is monosodium glutamate, the solid form of a natural amino acid found in many vegetables. It can be found in stores in the spice sections and as the brand name Accent Flavor Enhancer. MSG is an important component of several KFC items.

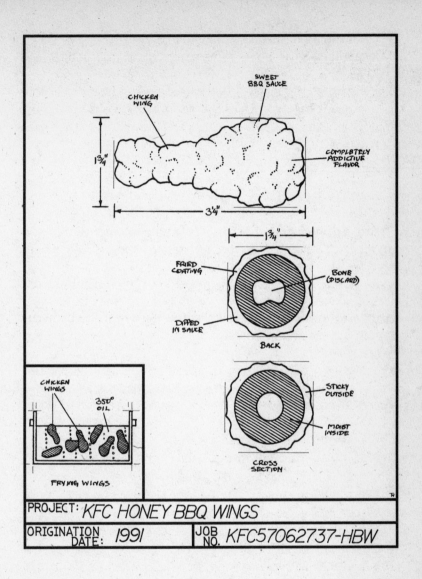

CHICKEN WING

SWEET BBQ SAUCE

COMPLETELY ADDICTIVE FLAVOR

1¾"

3¼"

1¾"

FRIED COATING

BONE (DISCARD)

DIPPED IN SAUCE

BACK

STICKY OUTSIDE

MOIST INSIDE

CROSS SECTION

CHICKEN WINGS

350° OIL

FRYING WINGS

PROJECT: *KFC HONEY BBQ WINGS*

ORIGINATION DATE: *1991*

JOB NO. *KFC57062737-HBW*

KFC
MACARONI & CHEESE

☆　　♥　　☎　　✎　　✈　　✉　　✂　　☛　　✿

Here's a clone for another of KFC's famous side dishes. We'll use easy-to-melt Velveeta, with its very smooth texture, as the main ingredient for the cheese sauce. Then a bit of cheddar cheese is added to give the sauce a sharp cheddary zing like the original. It's a very simple recipe that will take only 15 minutes to prepare. That's great news for impatient cooks who want to dig right into the tasty vittles. Weeell doggies!

6 cups water
1 1/3 cups elbow macaroni
4 ounces Velveeta cheese

1/2 cup shredded cheddar cheese
2 tablespoons whole milk
1/4 teaspoon salt

1. Bring water to a boil over high heat in a medium saucepan. Add elbow macaroni to the water and cook it for 10 to 12 minutes or until tender, stirring occasionally.
2. While the macaroni is boiling, prepare the cheese sauce by combining the remaining ingredients in a small saucepan over low heat. Stir often as the cheese melts into a smooth consistency.
3. When the macaroni is done, strain it and then pour it back into the same pan, without the water.
4. Add the cheese sauce to the pan and stir gently until the macaroni is well coated with the cheese. Serve immediately while hot.

• MAKES ABOUT 3 SERVINGS.

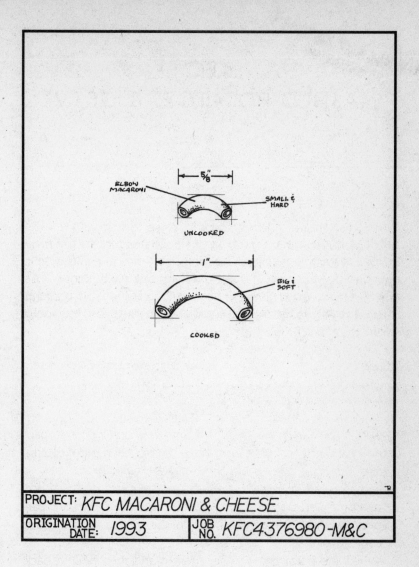

ELBOW
MACARONI

5⅛"

SMALL &
HARD

UNCOOKED

1"

BIG &
SOFT

COOKED

PROJECT: *KFC MACARONI & CHEESE*

ORIGINATION
DATE: *1993*

JOB
NO. *KFC4376980-M&C*

KFC
MASHED POTATOES & GRAVY

☆　♥　☎　✎　✈　✉　✄　☞　✿

This gravy recipe should come very close to that tasty tan stuff that's poured over the fluffy mashed potatoes at the Colonel's chain of restaurants. And since the original recipe contains MSG (as does their chicken), this clone was designed with that "secret" ingredient. You may choose to leave out the MSG, which is a natural amino acid found in vegetables and seaweed. But your clone won't taste exactly like the real thing without it.

GRAVY
1 tablespoon vegetable oil
4 ½ tablespoons all-purpose flour
1 can Campbell's chicken broth
　(plus 1 can water)
　(see Tidbits)
¼ teaspoon salt
⅛ teaspoon MSG or Accent Flavor
　Enhancer
⅛ teaspoon ground black pepper

MASHED POTATOES
1 ½ cups water
⅓ cup milk
3 tablespoons butter
½ teaspoon salt
1 ½ cups instant mashed potato
　flakes (Potato Buds)

1. First make a roux by combining the oil with 1 ½ tablespoons of flour in a medium saucepan over low to medium heat. Heat the mixture for 20 to 30 minutes, stirring often, until it is a chocolate color.
2. Remove the roux from the heat, add the remaining ingredients to the saucepan, and stir.

3. Put the saucepan back over the heat, turn it up to medium, and bring the gravy to a boil. Reduce heat and simmer for 10 to 15 minutes, or until thick.
4. As the gravy is reducing, prepare the potatoes by combining 1½ cups of water, ⅓ cup of milk, butter, and ½ teaspoon of salt in a medium saucepan over medium heat. Bring to a boil, then remove the pan from heat. Add the potato flakes, and whip with a fork until fluffy.
5. Serve the mashed potatoes with gravy poured over the top. As if you didn't know.

• MAKES 3 TO 4 SERVINGS.

TIDBITS

If Campbell's chicken broth is not available you can use 2½ cups of any chicken stock.

KFC
POTATO SALAD

☆　♥　☎　✆　✈　✉　✂　☞　✿

Here's a simple clone for the scrumptious potato salad that you get as a side dish from America's largest fast food chicken chain. Some of the skin is left on the potatoes in the real thing, so you don't have to peel them too thoroughly. Just be sure to chop your potatoes into cubes that are approximately ½ inch thick, and then let the salad marinate for at least 4 hours so that the flavors can properly develop. If you let the salad chill overnight, it tastes even better.

2 pounds russet potatoes
1 cup mayonnaise
4 teaspoons sweet pickle relish
4 teaspoons sugar
2 teaspoons minced white onion
2 teaspoons prepared mustard
1 teaspoon vinegar

1 teaspoon minced celery
1 teaspoon diced pimentos
½ teaspoon shredded carrot
¼ teaspoon dried parsley
¼ teaspoon pepper
dash salt

1. Lightly peel the potatoes (leave a little skin on), then chop them into bite-size pieces and boil in 6 cups of boiling, salted water for 7 to 10 minutes. The potato chunks should be tender, yet slightly tough in the middle when done. Drain and rinse potatoes with cold water.
2. In a medium bowl, combine remaining ingredients and whisk until smooth.

3. Pour drained potatoes into a large bowl. Pour the dressing over the potatoes and mix until well combined.
4. Cover and chill for at least 4 hours. Overnight is best.

• MAKES 6 CUPS (ABOUT 8 SERVINGS).

KRAFT
DELUXE MACARONI & CHEESE

☆　♥　☎　✎　✈　⊠　✂　☞　✿

It's time to clone America's best-selling brand of instant macaroni & cheese. This recipe is for the "Deluxe" variety of this popular product—that is, the one that comes with an envelope of thick cheese sauce, rather than the dry, powdered cheese. I think the "Deluxe" version, with its two-cheese blend, is the better tasting of the two, although it's gonna hit you a bit harder in the wallet at the supermarket. But now, with this Top Secret Recipe, you can make creamy macaroni & cheese that tastes like Kraft's original at a fraction of the price of the real deal. You gotta love that!

8 cups water
2 cups uncooked elbow macaroni
⅓ cup shredded cheddar cheese

½ cup Cheez Whiz
2 tablespoons whole milk
¼ teaspoon salt

1. Bring 8 cups (2 quarts) of water to a boil over high heat in a large saucepan. Add elbow macaroni to water and cook for 10 to 12 minutes or until tender, stirring occasionally.
2. As macaroni boils, prepare sauce by combining cheddar cheese, Cheez Whiz, and milk in a small saucepan over medium low heat. Stir cheese mixture often as it heats, so that it does not burn. Add salt. When all of the cheddar cheese has melted and the sauce is smooth, cover the pan and set it aside until macaroni is ready.

3. When macaroni is ready, strain the water, but do not rinse the macaroni.
4. Using the same pan you prepared the macaroni in, combine the macaroni with the cheese sauce, and mix well.

- MAKES ABOUT 4 CUPS.

KRAFT
SHAKE 'N BAKE

☆　♥　☎　✎　✈　✉　✂　☛　✿

Need a recipe that copies Shake 'n Bake in a pinch? Or maybe you don't feel like going to the store for the real thing. Here's the *TSR* solution for a quick clone that will give you the same texture and flavor of Kraft Shake 'n Bake using very common ingredients. You may notice the color is a bit different in this clone when compared to the real thing. That's because this recipe doesn't include beet powder—a hard-to-find ingredient that lends a dark orange tint to the original. But after you sink your teeth into this chicken (baked the same way as described on the Shake 'n Bake box) you'll swear it's the same stuff you buy in a box. When you're ready to get shaking and baking, use this breading on 2½ pounds of chicken pieces or on 2 pounds of skinless chicken breast fillets.

½ cup plus 1 tablespoon corn flake crumbs
2 teaspoons all-purpose flour
1 teaspoon salt
¼ teaspoon paprika
¼ teaspoon sugar
scant ¼ teaspoon garlic powder
scant ¼ teaspoon onion powder

1. Combine all ingredients in a small bowl and stir to combine.
2. Prepare chicken following the same technique as described on the box of the original mix using 2½ pounds of bone-in chicken (6 to 8 pieces, with or without skin) or 2 pounds boneless skinless chicken breast halves. Preheat your oven to 400 degrees, then moisten the chicken with water. Use a large plastic

bag for the coating and use the same steps as described on the original package:

"Shake moistened chicken, 1 to 2 pieces at a time, in shaker bag with coating mixture. Discard any remaining mixture and bag. Bake at 400 degrees in ungreased or foil-lined 15 × 10 × 1-inch baking pan until cooked through—bone-in: 45 minutes/boneless: 20 minutes."

• SERVES 4.

KRAFT
STOVE TOP STUFFING

☆ ♥ ☎ ✎ ✈ ✉ ✂ ☞ ✿

This recipe clones the common 6-ounce box of Stove Top stuffing mix you find in any market. This secret formula duplicates the chicken variety, the brand's most popular version. You know, it's nice to be able to make as much of this as you want prior to the holiday crunch and just keep it sealed up in the pantry until you're ready to use it. Besides, you have enough to worry about deciding which fruits to use in the Jell-O® mold. When it's time to cook, it's just a matter of adding some water and margarine to this mix, and in 10 easy minutes the stuff is all ready to go up a turkey's backside.

DRY MIX
1/3 cup minced fresh celery
4 to 5 slices white bread
3 to 4 slices wheat bread
3 chicken bouillon cubes, crushed
2 teaspoons dried chopped onions
1 1/2 teaspoons dried parsley

1/8 teaspoon sugar
1/8 teaspoon onion powder

TO MAKE STUFFING
1 2/3 cups water
1/4 cup margarine

1. Arrange the celery pieces on a plate and set the plate in a warm place—a sunny window is best—for 24 hours or until the celery is thoroughly dry. This is the best way to dry the tiny pieces of celery for the instant stuffing mix. You must be sure to remove all moisture from the celery. You should end up with 2 teaspoons of dried celery from 1/3 cup of freshly minced celery.

2. Prepare bread crumbs by stacking the bread slices on top of each other and squishing them down flat with the palms of your hands. This will create denser bread crumbs that will not become soggy and pasty when cooking. Use a sharp knife to dice the bread into little pieces. You should have about 2½ cups of white bread and 1½ cups of wheat for a total of around 4 cups of bread.
3. Preheat the oven to 250 degrees. Spread the bread crumbs on a cookie sheet. Bake for 30 to 40 minutes or until the bread is completely dry. You should now have around 2⅔ cups of dry bread crumbs.
4. To make the vegetable/seasoning mix, combine the dried celery with chicken bouillon powder, onions, parsley, sugar, and onion powder in a small bowl. You now have a stuffing kit that can be sealed up and stored in a dry place until you are ready to use it.
5. To make the stuffing, mix the vegetable/seasoning mix with 1⅔ cups water in a medium saucepan over medium heat. Bring the mixture to a boil, then reduce heat to low, cover, and simmer for 10 minutes. Stir in the bread crumbs, cover, and remove from heat. Let stuffing stand 5 to 7 minutes. Fluff it with a fork before serving.

• MAKES 6 SERVINGS.

KRAFT
THOUSAND ISLAND DRESSING

☆   ♥   ☎   ✎   ✈   ✉   ✂   ☞   ✿

Here's a quick clone for one of the best-selling thousand island dressings around. Use this one on salads or on burgers as a homemade "special sauce." It's easy, it's tasty, it's cheap ... and it can be made low fat simply by using light mayo. Dig it.

½ cup mayonnaise
2 tablespoons ketchup
1 tablespoon white vinegar
2 teaspoons sugar
2 teaspoons sweet pickle relish

1 teaspoon finely minced white
  onion
⅛ teaspoon salt
dash black pepper

1. Combine all of the ingredients in a small bowl. Stir well.
2. Place dressing in a covered container and refrigerate for several hours, stirring occasionally, so that the sugar dissolves and the flavors blend.

• MAKES ABOUT ¾ CUP.

LAWRY'S
SEASONED SALT

☆ ♥ ☎ ✎ ✈ ✉ ✂ ☛ ✿

This seven-ingredient clone of Lawry's Seasoned Salt can be made in a small bowl, but it's best stored in an old shaker-top spice bottle that you've cleaned out and saved. You've saved one of those somewhere, right?

2 tablespoons salt
2 teaspoons sugar
½ teaspoon paprika
¼ teaspoon turmeric

¼ teaspoon onion powder
¼ teaspoon garlic powder
¼ teaspoon cornstarch

1. Combine all ingredients in a small bowl and mix well.
2. Pour blend into an empty spice bottle with a shaker top to store.

• MAKES ¼ CUP.

LAWRY'S
TACO SPICES & SEASONING

☆　♥　☎　✎　✈　⊠　✂　☞　✿

This is a clone for the stuff you buy in 1-ounce packets to create, as the package says, "a fun-filled Mexican fiesta in minutes." Isn't that so true? In fact, thanks to Lawry's, my last Mexican fiesta was filled with so much pure fun that I had to take a siesta the next day. I owe it all to that fabulous little packet of seasoning. And now I promise you just as much super duper fun with this *TSR* clone. Golly, maybe even a tad more fun if you're lucky. Just mix the ingredients together in a small bowl, then add it to 1 pound of browned ground beef along with some water and let it simmer. Before you know it you'll be up to your nostrils in good old-fashioned, taco-making fun.

1 tablespoon flour	½ teaspoon cumin
1 teaspoon chili powder	¼ teaspoon cayenne pepper
1 teaspoon paprika	¼ teaspoon garlic powder
¾ teaspoon salt	¼ teaspoon sugar
¾ teaspoon minced onion	⅛ teaspoon ground oregano

1. Combine all of the ingredients in a small bowl.
2. To prepare the meat filling for the tacos as described on the original package instructions: "In large skillet, brown 1 pound ground beef until crumbly; drain fat. Add spices & seasoning and ⅔ cup water; mix thoroughly. Bring to a boil; reduce heat to low, and cook, uncovered, 7 to 10 minutes, stirring occasion-

ally. Spoon meat filling into warmed taco shells or tortillas. Top with shredded lettuce, grated cheddar cheese, and chopped tomato. Use fresh salsa and guacamole if desired."

• MAKES MEAT FILLING FOR 12 TACOS (ABOUT 3 TABLESPOONS EACH).

LITTLE DEBBIE
OATMEAL CREME PIES

☆　♥　☎　✎　✈　✉　✂　☛　✿

These soft, creme-filled sandwich cookies were the first snacks produced by McKee Foods back in 1960. It was his 4-year-old granddaughter Debbie after whom founder O.D. McKee named his line of snack cakes. O.D. was inspired by a picture of the little girl in play clothes and a straw hat, and that's the image we still find today on every package. The secret to cloning these mouth-watering snacks is re-creating the soft, chewy consistency of the oatmeal cookies. To duplicate the texture, the cookies are slightly under-baked. Then you whip up some of the easy-to-make creme filling with marshmallow creme and spread it between two of the oatmeal cookies to complete the sandwich. Next stop, yum city!

COOKIES

1 cup margarine
¾ cup dark brown sugar
½ cup sugar
1 tablespoon molasses
1 teaspoon vanilla
2 eggs
1½ cups all-purpose flour
½ teaspoon salt
1 teaspoon baking soda
⅛ teaspoon cinnamon
1½ cups 1-minute Quaker Oats

CREME FILLING

2 teaspoons very hot water
¼ teaspoon salt
2 cups marshmallow creme
　(one 7-ounce jar)
½ cup shortening
⅓ cup powdered sugar
½ teaspoon vanilla

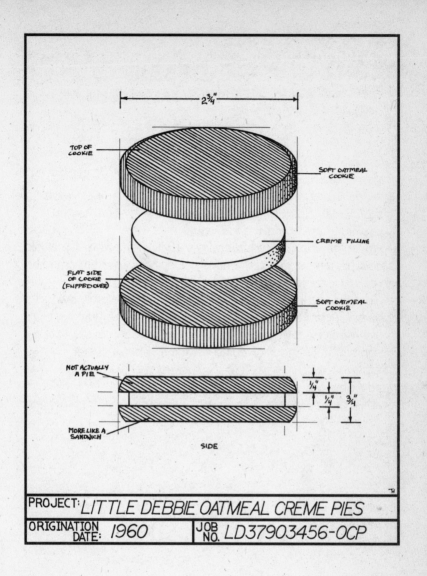

2¾"

TOP OF COOKIE

SOFT OATMEAL COOKIE

CREME FILLING

FLAT SIDE OF COOKIE (FLIPPED OVER)

SOFT OATMEAL COOKIE

NOT ACTUALLY A PIE

¼"
¼"
3¾"

MORE LIKE A SANDWICH

SIDE

PROJECT: *LITTLE DEBBIE OATMEAL CREME PIES*

ORIGINATION DATE: *1960*	JOB NO. *LD37903456-OCP*

1. Preheat oven to 350 degrees.
2. In a large bowl, cream together margarine, sugars, molasses, vanilla, and eggs.
3. In a separate bowl combine the flour, salt, baking soda, and cinnamon.
4. Combine the dry ingredients with the wet ingredients. Mix in the oats.
5. Drop dough by tablespoonfuls onto an ungreased baking sheet. Bake for 10 to 12 minutes, or until cookies are just starting to darken around the edges. They will still appear moist in the center. Be careful not to overcook—when cooled, the cookies should be soft and chewy.
6. While the cookies bake, prepare the filling. Use a small bowl to dissolve the salt in 2 teaspoons of very hot water. Set this solution aside to cool.
7. Combine the marshmallow creme, shortening, powdered sugar, and vanilla in a medium bowl and mix well with an electric mixer on high speed until fluffy. Add the cooled salt solution to the filling mixture and combine with the mixer.
8. Assemble each creme pie by spreading the filling over one side of a cookie (the flat side) and press another cookie on top, making a sandwich. Repeat for the remaining cookies and filling.

• MAKES 2 DOZEN CREME PIES.

MCDONALD'S
ARCH DELUXE

☆ ♥ ☎ ✎ ✈ ✉ ✂ ☞ ✿

In 1996, McDonald's set out to target more educated tastebuds in a massive advertising campaign for its newest burger creation. We watched while Ronald McDonald golfed, danced, and leisurely hung out with real-life grown-up humans, instead of the puffy Mayor McCheese and that bunch of wacko puppets. Supposedly the Arch Deluxe, with the "Adult Taste," would appeal to those golfers and dancers and anyone else with a sophisticated palate. But let's face it, we're not talking Beef Wellington here. The Arch Deluxe was just a hamburger, after all, with only a couple of elements that set it apart from the other menu items. The big difference was the creamy brown mustard spread on the sandwich right next to the ketchup. And the burger was assembled on a sesame seed potato roll (which actually tasted very much like your common hamburger bun). Also, you could order the burger with the optional thick-sliced peppered bacon, for an extra bit of ka-ching.

Okay, so the plan didn't quite work out the way Mickey D's had hoped. Sales of the Arch Deluxe were disappointing, to say the least. And shortly after the Arch Deluxe was unveiled it was but a figment of our drive-thru memory. That's why I thought this would be a good recipe to clone. You know, for all of you who have been struggling to get by without the Arch Deluxe in your lives. The Arch Deluxe may have gone on to join the McD.L.T. and the McLean Deluxe on the great list of fast food duds from our past. But you can now create a delicious kitchen facsimile of your own with this recipe. And hopefully, in the meantime, Ronald has gone back to work.

1 tablespoon mayonnaise
½ teaspoon brown mustard
   (French's "Hearty Deli" is good)
1 sesame seed hamburger bun
¼ pound ground beef

1 slice American cheese
1 to 2 tomato slices
1 to 2 lettuce leaves, chopped
½ tablespoon ketchup
2 tablespoons chopped onion

1. In a small bowl, mix together the mayonnaise and the brown mustard. Set aside.
2. Grill the face of each of the buns on a griddle or frying pan over medium heat.
3. Roll the ground beef into a ball and pat it out until it's approximately the same diameter as the bun.
4. Cook meat on hot griddle or frying pan for about 5 minutes per side or until done. Be sure to lightly salt and pepper each side of the patty.
5. Build the burger in the following order, from the bottom up:

ON BOTTOM BUN
beef patty
American cheese slice
1 to 2 tomato slices
lettuce

ON TOP BUN
mayo/mustard
ketchup
onions

6. Slap the top onto the bottom and serve hot.

• MAKES ONE BURGER.

TIDBITS

If you can find thick-sliced pepper bacon in your supermarket, you can add it to the burger just as you could at the restaurant chain. Cut one slice in half after cooking and place the slices next to each other onto the bottom bun before adding the beef patty.

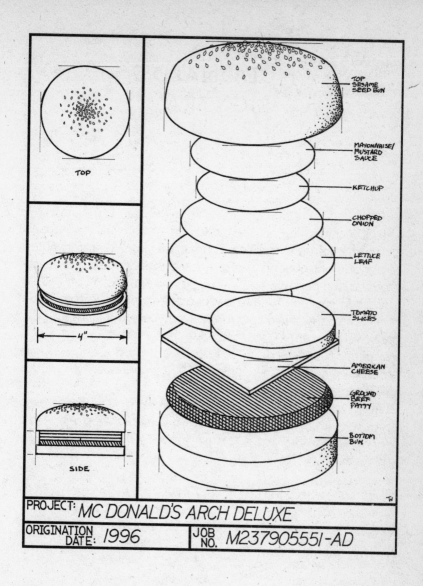

TOP

4"

SIDE

TOP
SESAME
SEED BUN

MAYONNAISE/
MUSTARD
SAUCE

KETCHUP

CHOPPED
ONION

LETTUCE
LEAF

TOMATO
SLICES

AMERICAN
CHEESE

GROUND
BEEF
PATTY

BOTTOM
BUN

PROJECT: *MC DONALD'S ARCH DELUXE*

ORIGINATION DATE: *1996*

JOB NO. *M23790555I-AD*

MCDONALD'S BIGXTRA!

☆   ♥   ☎   ✎   ✈   ✉   ✂   ☞   ✿

McDonald's roll-out of the BigXtra! is another bomb dropped on the battlefield of the latest burger war. Burger King took the first shot by introducing the Big King—a pretty good clone of McDonald's signature Big Mac, with a bit more meat and no middle bun. Then Mickey D's fired back with a clone of Burger King's popular Whopper hamburger, with, you guessed it, a bigger beef patty—20 percent bigger than the Whopper, to be exact. That's just under 5 ounces of ground beef, stacked on a huge sesame seed bun, with the same ingredients you would find piled on the Whopper—lettuce, onion, tomato, ketchup, mayo, and pickles. Plus McDonald's addition of a special spice sprinkled on the beef as it cooks. It's all very tasty. Especially if you like Whoppers.

Today the BigXtra! is less extra, having been shrunk down and renamed Big 'N Tasty.

1 large sesame seed bun	1 tablespoon mayonnaise
(4¾-inch diameter)	1 tablespoon chopped onion
5 ounces ground beef	3 pickle slices (hamburger style)
seasoned salt	½ cup chopped lettuce
ground black pepper	1 large tomato slice
2 teaspoons ketchup	non-stick cooking spray

1. Form the ground beef into a very large patty on wax paper. Make it approximately 5½ to 6 inches in diameter (the meat should shrink to the perfect size for the buns when cooked). Freeze this patty for a couple hours before cooking.

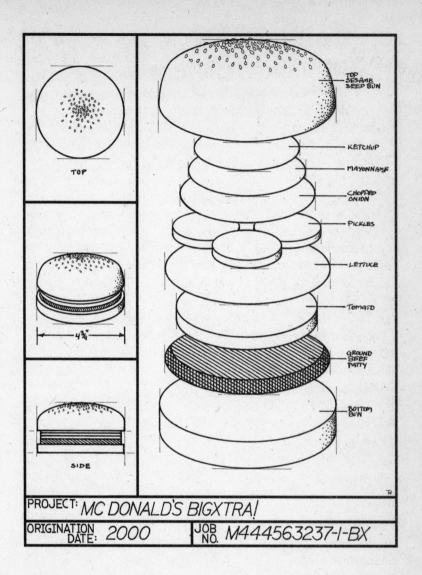

TOP

SIDE

4¾"

TOP
SESAME
SEED BUN

KETCHUP

MAYONNAISE

CHOPPED
ONION

PICKLES

LETTUCE

TOMATO

GROUND
BEEF
PATTY

BOTTOM
BUN

PROJECT: *MC DONALD'S BIGXTRA!*

ORIGINATION DATE: *2000*

JOB NO. *M444563237-1-BX*

2. Grill the faces of the hamburger bun in a hot skillet over medium heat. Grill until the buns are golden brown. Leave pan hot.
3. Grill the frozen patty in the pan for 2 to 3 minutes per side. Sprinkle one side with seasoned salt and ground black pepper.
4. Prepare the rest of the burger by first spreading the 2 teaspoons of ketchup on the face of the top bun. Follow the ketchup with the tablespoon of mayonnaise.
5. Stack the onion onto the top bun next, followed by the pickles and lettuce. Add the tomato slice to the top of the stack.
6. When the beef patty is done cooking, use a spatula to arrange it on the bottom bun. Turn the top of the burger over onto the bottom and serve.

- MAKES 1 HAMBURGER.

TIDBITS

If you want to add a slice of American cheese to your burger, it goes between the beef patty and bottom bun.

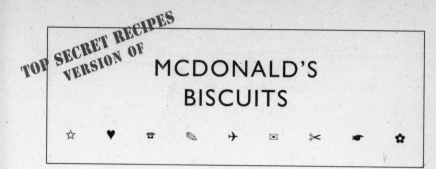

MCDONALD'S
BISCUITS

Them's the biscuits served at America's most popular stop for breakfast, partners—simple to make and gosh darn tasty. Get yourself some Bisquick and buttermilk and crank up the oven for a clone that's become one very frequent request.

2 cups Bisquick baking mix
⅔ cup buttermilk
2 teaspoons sugar

¼ teaspoon salt
2 tablespoons margarine, melted
   and divided

1. Preheat oven to 450 degrees.
2. Combine the baking mix, buttermilk, sugar, salt, and half of the melted margarine in a medium bowl. Mix until well blended.
3. Turn dough out onto a floured surface and knead for about 30 seconds, or until dough becomes elastic.
4. Roll dough to about ¾ inch thick and punch out biscuits using a 3-inch cutter. Arrange the punched-out dough on an ungreased baking sheet, and bake for 10 to 12 minutes or until the biscuits are golden on top and have doubled in height.
5. Remove the biscuits from the oven and immediately brush each one with a light coating of the remaining melted margarine. Serve warm.

• MAKES 8 BISCUITS.

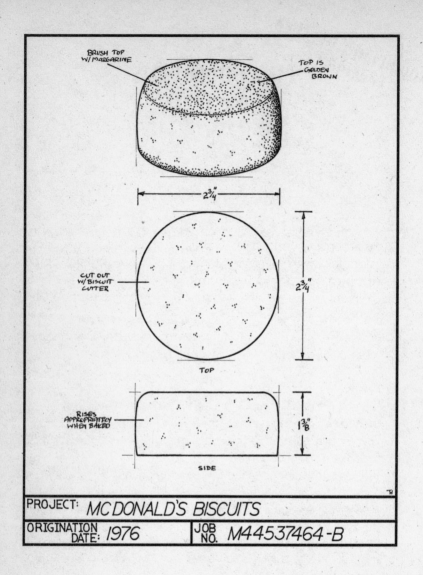

BRUSH TOP
W/MARGARINE

TOP IS
GOLDEN
BROWN

2¾"

CUT OUT
W/BISCUIT
CUTTER

2¾"

TOP

RISES
APPROPRIATELY
WHEN BAKED

1⅜"

SIDE

PROJECT: *MCDONALD'S BISCUITS*

ORIGINATION
DATE: *1976*

JOB
NO. *M44537464-B*

MCDONALD'S BREAKFAST BAGEL SANDWICHES

☆　♥　☎　✎　✈　⊠　✂　☛　✿

Hold an entire breakfast in two hands and bring it right up to your face for a bite. Here are clones for all three varieties of the newest breakfast sandwiches from the Golden Arches. The only requirement is that you have a small 6-inch skillet to make the omelette for each sandwich. Take your pick.

HAM & EGG BAGEL

SAUCE
2 tablespoons mayonnaise
1 teaspoon creamy dill mustard

4 eggs
salt
ground black pepper

1 teaspoon butter
8 ounces deli-sliced ham (2 to 3 slices per sandwich)
4 plain bagels
8 slices Kraft Singles American cheese

1. First prepare the sauce by combining the mayonnaise with the dill mustard in a small bowl. Set this aside until you are ready to use it.
2. To prepare the eggs it's best to make one at a time in a small 6-inch skillet. If you have more than one of these small pans, you can save a little time.
3. Beat an egg in a small bowl with a whisk until it is smooth, but not foamy. Add a pinch of salt and pepper to the egg. Heat a

small 6-inch skillet over low heat. Add ¼ teaspoon of butter to the pan. When the butter has melted add the egg to the pan. Swirl the pan so that the egg spreads evenly. As the egg begins to cook, use a spatula to pull in a couple of the edges so that raw egg flows from the top onto the hot pan. Cook for 2 to 3 minutes, then fold over one of the edges of the egg using a spoon or fork. Fold it down about an inch. Fold the opposite end over as well. Then fold the remaining two edges over, creating a small rectangular or square mini-omelette. Flip the little omelette over and turn off the heat.

4. Heat up the ham in a covered dish in the microwave for 1 minute. This will make it hot, and keep it from drying.

5. Slice a bagel in half and place it with the faces up on a baking sheet. Grill the faces of the bagel halves in your oven, set on broil, until golden brown. You may also use a toaster oven for this step, but be sure to place the sliced bagel halves onto a small baking sheet or on aluminum foil so that only the faces are toasted.

6. When the bagels are toasted, spread about ½ tablespoon of the sauce onto the face of the top bagel half.

7. Place a slice of cheese onto the face of each bagel half.

8. Place the finished omelette onto the cheese on the bottom half of the sandwich.

9. Place the ham onto the egg.

10. Finish by flipping the top half of the sandwich over onto the bottom. Heat for 15 seconds in microwave if needed to warm.

• MAKES 4 SERVINGS.

STEAK & EGG BAGEL

SAUCE
2 tablespoons mayonnaise
1 teaspoon creamy dill mustard

1 teaspoon vegetable oil

1 slice white onion, quartered
One 14-ounce package Steak-
    Umm chopped steak (7 steaks)
4 eggs
1 teaspoon butter

salt

ground black pepper

4 plain bagels

8 slices Kraft Singles American cheese

1. First prepare the sauce by combining the mayonnaise with the dill mustard in a small bowl. Set this aside until you are ready to use it.
2. Heat 1 teaspoon of vegetable oil in a medium skillet over medium heat. Separate the onion slices and sauté in the oil until light brown.
3. Heat a large skillet over medium high heat. Break up the sandwich steak into the hot pan and cook until brown. Drain off fat. Add the grilled onions to the meat and stir.
4. To make the eggs it's best to make one at a time in a small 6-inch skillet. If you have more than one of these small pans, you can save a little time.
5. Beat an egg in a small bowl with a whisk until it is smooth, but not foamy. Add a pinch of salt and pepper to the egg. Heat a small 6-inch skillet over low heat. Add ¼ teaspoon of butter to the pan. When the butter has melted add the egg to the pan. Swirl the pan so that the egg spreads evenly. As the egg begins to cook, use a spatula to pull in a couple of the edges so that raw egg flows from the top onto the hot pan. Cook for 2 to 3 minutes, then fold over one of the edges of the egg using a spoon or fork. Fold it down about an inch. Fold the opposite end over as well. Then fold the remaining two edges over, creating a small rectangular or square mini-omelette. Flip the little omelette over and turn off the heat.
6. Slice a bagel in half and place it with the faces up on a baking sheet. Grill the faces of the bagel halves in your oven, set on broil, until golden brown. You may also use a toaster oven for this step, but be sure to place the sliced bagel halves onto a small baking sheet or on aluminum foil so that only the faces are toasted.
7. When the bagels are toasted, spread about ½ tablespoon of the sauce onto the face of the top bagel half.
8. Place a slice of cheese onto the face of each bagel half.

9. Divide the meat into four portions and stack one portion onto the cheese on the bottom bagel half.

10. Place the finished omelette onto the meat on the bottom half of the sandwich.

11. Finish by flipping the top half of the sandwich over onto the bottom. Heat for 15 seconds in microwave if needed to warm.

- MAKES 4 SERVINGS.

SPANISH OMELET BAGEL

SAUCE
2 tablespoons mayonnaise
1 teaspoon creamy dill mustard
2 teaspoons minced green pepper
2 teaspoons minced white onion
4 eggs
1 teaspoon butter
salt

ground black pepper
8 ounces breakfast sausage

4 plain bagels
4 slices Kraft Singles American cheese
4 slices Kraft Singles Monterey Jack cheese

1. First prepare the sauce by combining the mayonnaise with the dill mustard in a small bowl. Set this aside until you are ready to use it.

2. To prepare the eggs it's best to make one at a time in a small 6-inch skillet. If you have more than one of these small pans, you can save a little time.

3. First preheat pan over low heat. Add ¼ teaspoon of butter. Add ½ teaspoon of minced green pepper along with ½ teaspoon of minced white onion to the pan and sauté for a couple minutes, or until soft.

4. Beat an egg in a small bowl with a whisk until it is smooth, but not foamy. Add a pinch of salt and pepper to the egg. Add the egg to the pan with the vegetables. Swirl the pan so that the egg spreads out. As the egg begins to cook, use a spatula to pull in a couple of the edges so that raw egg flows from the top onto the hot pan. Cook for 2 to 3 minutes, then fold over

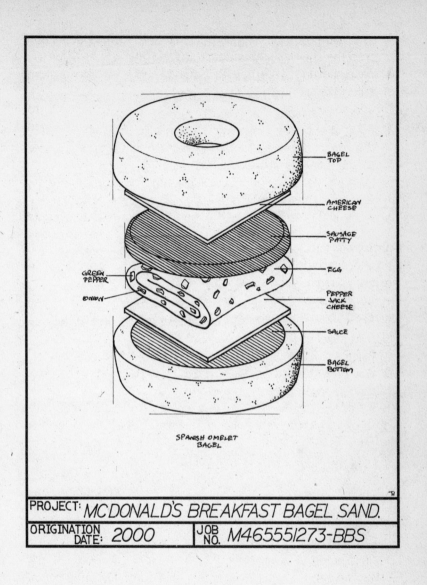

BAGEL
TOP

AMERICAN
CHEESE

SAUSAGE
PATTY

EGG

GREEN
PEPPER

ONION

PEPPER
JACK
CHEESE

SAUCE

BAGEL
BOTTOM

SPANISH OMELET
BAGEL

PROJECT:	*MCDONALD'S BREAKFAST BAGEL SAND.*	
ORIGINATION DATE: *2000*	JOB NO.	*M465551273-BBS*

135

one of the edges of the egg using a spoon or fork. Fold it down about an inch. Fold the opposite end over as well. Then fold the remaining two edges over, creating a small rectangular or square mini-omelette. Flip the little omelette over and turn off the heat.

5. Press the sausage into four 2-ounce patties approximately the size of the bagel. Cook the sausage in a large skillet over medium heat until brown. Drain when done.

6. Slice a bagel in half and place it with the faces up on a baking sheet. Grill the faces of the bagel halves in your oven, set on broil, until golden brown. You may also use a toaster oven for this step, but be sure to place the sliced bagel halves onto a small baking sheet or on aluminum foil so that only the faces are toasted.

7. When the bagels are toasted, spread about ½ tablespoon of the sauce onto the face of the bottom bagel half.

8. Place a slice of Monterey Jack cheese on the face of the bottom bagel half.

9. Place a sausage patty on the Jack cheese.

10. Place the finished omelette onto the sausage and then place the American cheese on the omelette.

11. Finish the sandwich with the bagel top and heat for 15 seconds in microwave if needed to warm. Repeat for remaining servings.

• MAKES 4 SERVINGS.

MCDONALD'S
BREAKFAST BURRITO

☆ ♥ ☎ ✎ ✈ ✉ ✂ ☛ ✿

It was in the late seventies, shortly after McDonald's had intro-duced the Egg McMuffin, that the food giant realized the potential of a quick, drive-thru breakfast. Soon, the company had devel-oped several breakfast selections, including the Big Breakfast with eggs, hash browns, and sausage, and this morning meal in a tor-tilla, first offered on the menu in 1991.

4 ounces breakfast sausage
1 tablespoon minced white onion
½ tablespoon minced mild green
   chilies (canned)
4 eggs, beaten
salt

pepper
4 8-inch flour tortillas
4 slices American cheese

ON THE SIDE
salsa

1. Preheat a skillet over medium heat. Crumble the sausage into the pan, then add the onion. Sauté the sausage and onion for 3 to 4 minutes or until the sausage is browned.
2. Add the mild green chilies and continue to sauté for 1 minute.
3. Pour the beaten eggs into the pan and scramble the eggs with the sausage and vegetables. Add a dash of salt and pepper.
4. Heat up the tortillas by steaming them in the microwave in moist paper towels or a tortilla steamer for 20 to 30 seconds.
5. Break each slice of cheese in half and position two halves end-to-end in the middle of each tortilla.
6. To make the burrito, spoon ¼ of the egg filling onto the cheese in a tortilla. Fold one side of the tortilla over the filling,

then fold up about 2 inches of one end. Fold over the other side of the tortilla to complete the burrito (one end should remain open). Serve hot with salsa on the side, if desired.

- MAKES 4 BURRITOS.

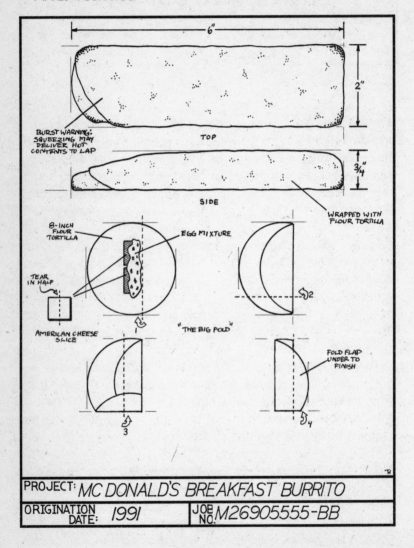

BURST WARNING: SQUEEZING MAY DELIVER HOT CONTENTS TO LAP

TOP

WRAPPED WITH FLOUR TORTILLA

SIDE

8-INCH FLOUR TORTILLA

EGG MIXTURE

TEAR IN HALF

AMERICAN CHEESE SLICE

"THE BIG FOLD"

FOLD FLAP UNDER TO FINISH

PROJECT: MC DONALD'S BREAKFAST BURRITO

ORIGINATION DATE: 1991

JOB NO. M26905555-BB

MCDONALD'S
FRENCH FRIES

☆　♥　☎　✎　✈　✉　✂　☛　✿

They're the world's most famous french fries, responsible for one-third of all U.S. french fry sales, and many would say they're the best. These fried spud strips are so popular that Burger King even changed its own recipe to better compete with the secret formula from Mickey D's. One quarter of all meals served today in American restaurants come with fries; a fact that thrills restaurateurs since fries are the most profitable menu item in the food industry. Proper preparation steps were developed by McDonald's to minimize in-store preparation time, while producing a fry that is soft on the inside and crispy on the outside. To achieve this same level of texture and taste our clone requires a two-step frying technique: Once before the fries are frozen, and then once afterward before serving. Be sure to use a slicer to cut the fries for a consistent thickness (¼ inch is perfect) and for a cooking result that will make them just like the real thing. McDonald's uses a minuscule amount of beef fat in the blanching stage when preparing the french fries. But we can still get away with a great-tasting clone without having to add lard to our recipe. In the stores the chain uses only vegetable fat for the final frying step.

2 large russet potatoes
One 48-ounce can shortening
salt

RECOMMENDED
Potato slicer

1. Peel the potatoes, dry them, and slice using a mandolin or other slicer with a setting as close to ¼-inch-square strips as

you've got. If your fries are a little thicker than ¼ inch the recipe will still work, but you definitely don't want super thick steak fries here.

2. Rinse the fries in a large bowl filled with around 8 cups of cold water. The water should become milky. Dump the water out and add another 8 cups of cold water plus some ice and let the fries sit for an hour.

3. Spoon the shortening into your deep fryer and turn to 375 degrees. On many fryers this is the highest setting.

4. Remove the fries from the water and spread them out on a paper towel to dry for 10 to 15 minutes. Don't let them sit much longer than this or they will begin to turn brown.

5. The shortening should now be hot enough for the blanching stage. Add bunches of the fries to the shortening for 1½ minutes at a time. Watch them carefully to be sure they don't begin to brown. If they start to brown on the edges, take 'em out. Remove the fries to a paper towel or metal rack to drain and cool. When the fries have cooled, put them into a resealable bag or covered container and freeze for 4 to 5 hours or until the potatoes are completely frozen. As the fries freeze you can turn off the fryer, but turn it back on and give it plenty of time to heat up before the final frying stage.

6. Split up the frozen fries and add one half at a time to the hot shortening. Fry for 4½ to 6 minutes or until the fries have become a golden brown color and are crispy on the outside when cool. The second batch may take a tad longer than the first, since the shortening may have cooled. Drain the fries to paper towels or a metal rack and salt generously.

- MAKES 4 SERVINGS.

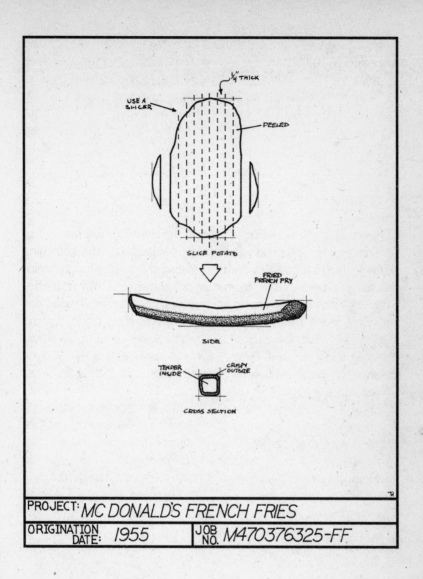

USE A SLICER

¼" THICK

PEELED

SLICE POTATO

SIDE

FRIED FRENCH FRY

TENDER INSIDE

CRISPY OUTSIDE

CROSS SECTION

TW

PROJECT: MC DONALD'S FRENCH FRIES

ORIGINATION DATE: 1955

JOB NO. M470376325-FF

MCDONALD'S
HOT MUSTARD SAUCE

☆　♥　☎　✎　✈　✉　✂　☞　✿

I finally got on the case to bring you the definitive kitchen clone for this one—and it's a cinch! Tie one hand behind your back and witness plain old ground dried mustard mixing it up with sweet and sour flavors in a saucepan over medium heat. The cornstarch wrangles around in there to thicken and stabilize while Captain Habanero pops in for the perfect spicy punch. Use it for dipping, use it for spreading ... use it again and again, since you'll make about a cup of the stuff. And McDonald's will be glad that we no longer need to hoard the little blister packs from the restaurants.

½ cup water
½ cup corn syrup
⅓ cup plus 1 tablespoon white vinegar
2 tablespoons ground dried mustard
4 teaspoons cornstarch

1 tablespoon granulated sugar
1 tablespoon vegetable oil
½ teaspoon turmeric
½ teaspoon salt
10 to 14 drops habanero hot sauce

1. Combine all ingredients in a small uncovered saucepan. Whisk until smooth.
2. Turn heat to medium and bring mixture to a boil, stirring often. Sauce should thicken in 2 to 3 minutes after it begins to boil. Remove sauce from heat and chill in refrigerator in a covered container.

• MAKES 1 CUP.

MCDONALD'S
SPECIAL SAUCE

☆   ♥   ☎   ✎   ✈   ✉   ✂   ☞   ✿

If you like Big Macs, it's probably because of that tasty "secret" spread that is plopped onto both decks of the world's most popular double-decker hamburger. So what's so special about this sauce? After all, it's basically just thousand island dressing, right? Pretty much. But this sauce has a bit more sweet pickle relish in it than a typical thousand island salad slather. Also, I found that this clone comes close to the original with the inclusion of French dressing. It's an important ingredient—ketchup just won't do it. That, along with a sweet & sour flavor that comes from vinegar and sugar, makes this sauce go well on any of your home burger creations, whether they're Big Mac clones or not. This is the closest "special sauce" clone you'll find ... anywhere.

½ cup mayonnaise
2 tablespoons French dressing
4 teaspoons sweet pickle relish
1 tablespoon finely minced white
  onion

1 teaspoon white vinegar
1 teaspoon sugar
⅛ teaspoon salt

1. Combine all of the ingredients in a small bowl. Stir well.
2. Place sauce in a covered container and refrigerate for several hours, or overnight, so that the flavors blend. Stir the sauce a couple of times as it chills.

• MAKES ABOUT ¾ CUP.

MCDONALD'S SWEET & SOUR DIPPING SAUCE

☆ ♥ ☎ ✎ ✈ ✉ ✂ ☛ ✿

This recipe clones one of those sauces you get with your order of McNuggets at the world's largest hamburger outlet. Now, instead of shoving a fistful of the little green packs into your backpack, you can make up a batch of your own to use as a dip for store-bought nuggets, chicken fingers, fried shrimp, and tempura. It's a simple recipe that requires a food processor or a blender, and the sauce will keep well for some time in the fridge.

¼ cup peach preserves
¼ cup apricot preserves
2 tablespoons light corn syrup
5 teaspoons white vinegar
1 ½ teaspoons cornstarch

½ teaspoon soy sauce
½ teaspoon yellow mustard
¼ teaspoon salt
⅛ teaspoon garlic powder
2 tablespoons water

1. Combine all ingredients except the water in a food processor or a blender and puree until the mixture is smooth.
2. Pour mixture into a small saucepan over medium heat. Add water, stir, and bring mixture to a boil. Allow it to boil for 5 minutes, stirring often. When the sauce has thickened, remove it from the heat and let it cool. Store sauce in a covered container in the refrigerator.

• MAKES ABOUT ¾ CUP.

MCDONALD'S YOGURT PARFAIT

☆　♥　☎　✎　✈　✉　✂　☞　✿

This one's super easy to make, plus it's low fat and delicious. The yogurt in the original is very sweet and creamy, like Yoplait. So that's the brand that you should use, although any brand of vanilla yogurt will work fine. If you use Yoplait, you'll need two 6-ounce containers of the stuff per serving. For the granola, just look for one that contains mostly oats. It should be crunchy and sweet (such as "maple" flavor) and can also include puffed rice bits. You can even make these a day or two ahead of time. Keep them covered in the fridge, and hold off on the granola topping until you serve 'em up or it'll get mighty soggy.

4 cups vanilla-flavored low-fat yogurt (or eight 6-ounce containers Yoplait)
Two 10-ounce boxes sliced frozen strawberries with sugar added, thawed

⅓ cup frozen blueberries, thawed
½ cup crunchy, sweet granola

1. Pour ½ cup of yogurt into a parfait cup or tall glass.
2. Add ½ cup of strawberries into the glass on top of the yogurt.
3. Add 1 tablespoon of blueberries to the glass.
4. Pour ½ cup of yogurt over the fruit.
5. Sprinkle granola over the top and serve. Repeat for remaining 3 servings.

• MAKES 4 SERVINGS.

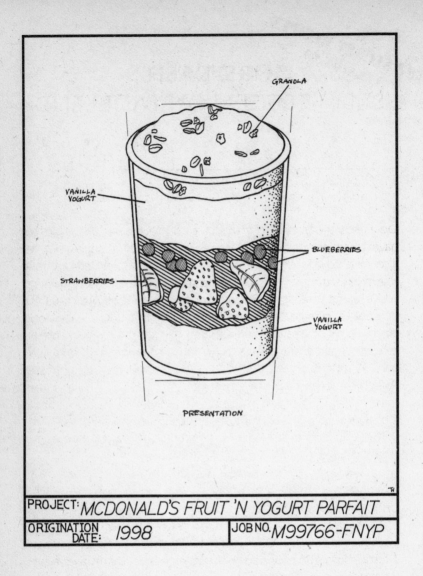

GRANOLA

VANILLA YOGURT

BLUEBERRIES

STRAWBERRIES

VANILLA YOGURT

PRESENTATION

PROJECT:	MCDONALD'S FRUIT 'N YOGURT PARFAIT
ORIGINATION DATE: 1998	JOB NO. M99766-FNYP

MRS. DASH
SALT-FREE SEASONING BLEND

☆　♥　☎　✎　✈　✉　✂　☞　✿

So here's the challenge with this clone recipe: Not only do we have to get the right ratios for nearly 20 different spices, but we also have to come up with a way to get the same lemony tang that makes the real Mrs. Dash the tasty salt-free seasoning blend we've come to know and love over the years. Sure, we could use powdered citric acid that is sometimes found in health food stores, but not everyone is going to have that ingredient readily available. Then we still need to figure out the "lemon juice solids" part. Ah, but wait, there's citric acid *and* lemon juice solids in Kool-Aid unsweetened lemonade drink mix. It's perfect! Add a little of that drink powder to the spice blend and we have a clone that in a blindfold taste test could fool even Mr. Dash.

¼ cup crushed dried minced
　onion flakes (see Tidbits)
4 teaspoons crushed dried
　vegetable flakes (Schilling)
　(see Tidbits)
1 tablespoon garlic powder
1 tablespoon dried orange peel
2 teaspoons coarse ground black
　pepper
1 teaspoon dried parsley
½ teaspoon dried basil
½ teaspoon dried marjoram

½ teaspoon dried oregano
½ teaspoon dried savory
½ teaspoon dried thyme
½ teaspoon cayenne pepper
½ teaspoon cumin
½ teaspoon coriander
½ teaspoon dried mustard
¼ teaspoon celery seed
¼ teaspoon Kool-Aid unsweet-
　ened lemonade drink mix
dash crushed dried rosemary

1. Combine all of the ingredients in a small bowl and stir well. As you stir, crush the leafy spices for a finer blend.
2. Store the spice blend in a covered container or a sealed shaker bottle.

- MAKES ABOUT ⅔ CUP.

TIDBITS

It's best to use a mortar and pestle to crush these sometimes tough little onion and vegetable flakes to about the size of rice, before adding them to the mix. But if you don't have one of those handy kitchen tools, you may also use the back of a spoon and a small bowl—plus a little grease. You know, the elbow kind.

NABISCO CHEESE NIPS

☆ ♥ ☎ ✎ ✈ ✉ ✂ ☛ ✿

Here's a clone recipe that gets one very important ingredient from another packaged product. The powdered cheese included in the Kraft instant macaroni & cheese kits flavors this homegrown version of the popular bright orange crackers. You'll need a can of Kraft Macaroni & Cheese Cheese Topping or two boxes of the most inexpensive instant variety of macaroni & cheese; you know, the kind with the cheese powder. Two boxes will give you enough cheese to make 300 crackers. As for the macaroni left over in the boxes, just use that for another recipe requiring elbow macaroni.

1 cup sifted all-purpose flour (plus
    ½ cup divided and reserved for
    kneading and rolling)
1 teaspoon baking soda
¼ teaspoon baking powder
½ cup Kraft Macaroni & Cheese
    Cheese Topping powder (or 2
    packages dry cheese powder
    from 2 boxes Kraft Macaroni &
    Cheese)

3 tablespoons shortening
⅓ cup buttermilk
½ teaspoon salt (for tops,
    optional)

1. Sift together 1 cup flour, baking soda, baking powder, and cheese powder in a large bowl.
2. Cut in the shortening with a fork and knife with a crosswise motion until dough is broken down into rice-size pieces. Mixture will still be very dry.

3. Stir in buttermilk with a fork until dough becomes very moist and sticky.

4. Sprinkle a couple tablespoons of the reserved flour over the dough and work it in until the dough can be handled without sticking, then turn it out onto a floured board, being sure to keep ¼ cup of the reserve flour for later. Knead the dough well for 60 to 90 seconds, until the flour is well incorporated. Wrap the dough in plastic wrap and chill for at least one hour.

5. Preheat oven to 325 degrees. Spray a light coating of cooking spray on a baking sheet.

6. Remove the dough from the refrigerator and use the remaining reserve flour to dust a rolling surface. Roll about one-third of the dough to just under 1/16 of an inch thick. Trim the edges square (a pizza cutter or wheel works great for this), then transfer the dough to a lightly greased baking sheet. Use the rolling pin to transfer the dough. Simply pick up one end of the dough onto a rolling pin, and roll the dough around the rolling pin. Reverse the process onto the baking sheet to transfer the dough.

7. Use a pizza cutter to cut across and down the dough, creating 1-inch-square pieces. Use the blunt end of a skewer or broken toothpick to poke a hole in the center of each piece.

8. Sprinkle a very light coating of salt over the top of the crackers (crackers will already be quite salty) and bake for 8 to 10 minutes. Mix the crackers around (so those on the edge don't burn) and bake for another 3 to 5 minutes, or until some are just barely turning a light brown. Repeat the rolling and baking process with the remaining dough.

- MAKES APPROXIMATELY 300 CRACKERS.

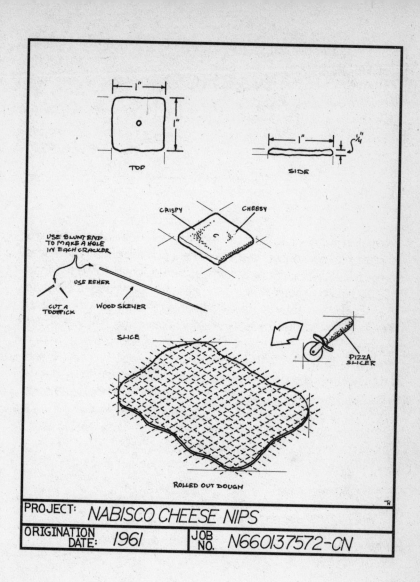

1"

1"

TOP

1"

$\frac{1}{4}$"

SIDE

CRISPY   CHEESY

USE BLUNT END
TO MAKE A HOLE
IN EACH CRACKER

USE EITHER

CUT A
TOOTHPICK

WOOD SKEWER

SLICE

PIZZA
SLICER

ROLLED OUT DOUGH

PROJECT: NABISCO CHEESE NIPS

ORIGINATION
DATE: 1961

JOB
NO. N660137572-CN

151

NABISCO
NILLA WAFERS

☆　　♥　　☎　　✎　　✈　　✉　　✂　　☞　　✿

No one knows the exact origin of the vanilla wafer but it's guessed that the recipe was developed in the South. The wafers were being created from scratch at home long before Nabisco introduced the lightweight, poker chip-like packaged cookies in 1945. Back then they were called Vanilla Wafers. But in the 60s Nabisco slapped the trade name Nilla Wafers on the box. Today the real things come about 100 to a box and really fly when whipped into the air with a little flick of the wrist. Here now, you can relive the days of old with a homemade version fresh out of the oven. This clone recipe makes about half a box's worth and they fly just as far.

For just a slight variation on this recipe—with similar aerodynamics—check out Sunshine Lemon Coolers on page 174.

½ cup powdered sugar
⅓ cup sugar
⅓ cup shortening
1 egg
1 teaspoon vanilla

⅛ teaspoon salt
1½ cups cake flour
1½ teaspoons baking powder
1 tablespoon water

1. Preheat oven to 325 degrees.
2. Cream together sugars, shortening, egg, vanilla, and salt in a large bowl.
3. Add the flour and baking powder. Add 1 tablespoon of water and continue mixing until dough forms a ball.

4. Roll dough into ¾-inch balls and flatten slightly onto a lightly greased cookie sheet. Bake for 15 to 18 minutes or until cookies are light brown.

- MAKES 50 TO 60 COOKIES.

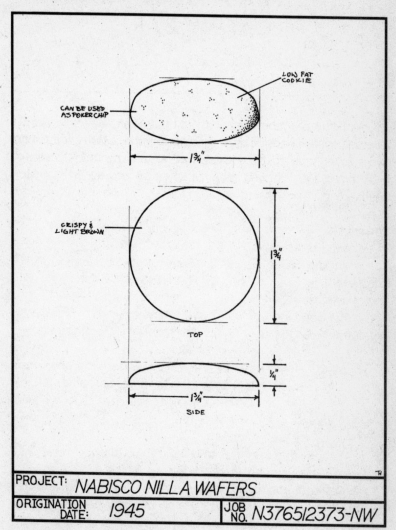

LOW FAT COOKIE

CAN BE USED AS POKER CHIP

1¾"

CRISPY & LIGHT BROWN

1¾"

TOP

¼"

1¾"

SIDE

PROJECT: NABISCO NILLA WAFERS

ORIGINATION DATE: 1945

JOB NO. N376512373-NW

NESTLÉ
BABY RUTH
CANDY BAR

☆　♥　☎　✍　✈　✉　✂　☞　✿

Beneath the chocolate of Nestlé's popular candy bar is a chewy, peanut-covered center that resembles Hershey's PayDay. To clone this one we'll only have to make a couple adjustments to that aforementioned recipe (found on page 83), then add the milk chocolate coating.

CENTERS

1/4 cup whole milk
5 unwrapped caramels
1 tablespoon light corn syrup
1 teaspoon butter
1/4 teaspoon vanilla
1/8 teaspoon salt

1 1/4 cups powdered sugar

20 unwrapped caramels
1 1/2 teaspoons water
2 cups dry roasted peanuts
1 12-ounce bag milk chocolate chips

1. Combine all ingredients for the centers, except the powdered sugar, in a small saucepan over low heat. Stir often as the caramel slowly melts. When the mixture is smooth, add 3/4 cup of powdered sugar. Stir. Save the remaining 1/2 cup of powdered sugar for later.

2. Use a candy thermometer to bring the mixture to exactly 230 degrees, stirring often, then turn off the heat.

3. When the temperature of the candy begins to drop, add the remaining 1/2 cup powdered sugar to the pan, then use a hand mixer on high speed to combine. Keep mixing until the candy cools and thickens and can no longer be mixed. That should take a minute or two.

4. Let the candy cool in the pan for 10 to 15 minutes, or until it can be touched. Don't let it sit too long—you want the candy to still be warm and pliable when you shape it. Take a tablespoon-size portion and roll it between your palms or on a countertop until it forms a roll the width of your index finger, and measuring about 4½ inches long. Repeat with the remaining center candy mixture and place the rolls on wax paper. You should have 8 rolls. Let the center rolls sit out for an hour or two to firm up.

5. Combine the 20 caramels with the 1½ teaspoons of water in a small saucepan over low heat. Stir often until the caramels melt completely, then turn off the heat. If you work fast this caramel will stay warm while you make the candy bars.

6. Pour the peanuts onto a baking sheet or other flat surface. Using a basting brush and working quickly, "paint" a coating of caramel onto one side of a center roll. Quickly turn the center over, caramel side down, onto the peanuts and press gently so that the peanuts stick to the surface of the candy. Paint more caramel onto the other side of the roll and press it down onto the peanuts. The candy should have a solid layer of peanuts covering all sides. If needed, brush additional caramel onto the roll, then turn it onto the peanuts to coat the roll completely. Place the candy bar onto wax paper, and repeat with the remaining ingredients. Place these bars into your refrigerator for an hour or two so that they firm up.

7. Pour the milk chocolate chips into a glass or ceramic bowl and zap it in the microwave for 2 minutes on 50 percent power. Gently stir the chips, then heat for an additional 30 seconds at 50 percent power. Repeat if necessary, stirring gently after each 30 seconds. Don't overcook the chips or the chocolate will burn and seize up on you.

8. Drop a candy bar center into the melted milk chocolate. Cover the candy bar with chocolate using two forks, one in each hand. When the candy is covered with chocolate, balance the bar on both of the forks, one at each end of the candy bar, and tap the forks on the top edge of the bowl so that much of the chocolate drops off. Carefully place the candy bar onto

wax paper and remove the two forks. Repeat with the remaining ingredients, and then chill the candy bars until firm.

• MAKES 8 CANDY BARS.

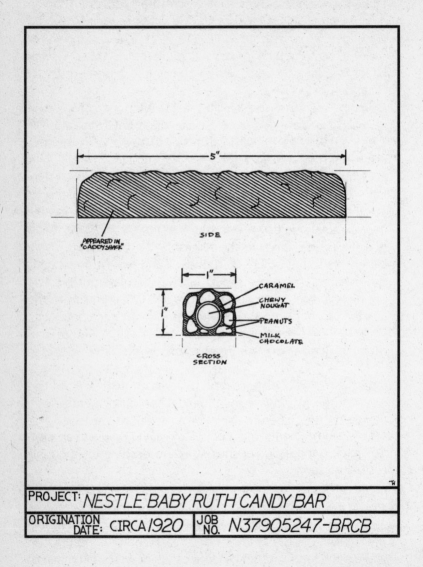

5"

SIDE

APPEARED IN "CADDYSHACK"

1"

1"

CARAMEL

CHEWY NOUGAT

PEANUTS

MILK CHOCOLATE

CROSS SECTION

PROJECT: NESTLE BABY RUTH CANDY BAR

ORIGINATION DATE: CIRCA 1920

JOB NO. N37905247-BRCB

NEWMAN'S OWN
CREAMY CAESAR DRESSING

☆ ♥ ☎ ✎ ✈ ✉ ✂ ☛ ✿

With over 100 million dollars given to charity since 1982, Newman's Own products have become an American favorite. One variety of the brand's dressings that really stands out is this exceptional Caesar salad dressing, probably the best commercial Caesar dressing on the market. Part of the secret for this special recipe is the inclusion of Worcestershire sauce. The sauce adds a beautiful flavor and color to the dressing, and contains a crucial fishy ingredient: anchovies.

1 cup mayonnaise
3 tablespoons distilled white
    vinegar
2 tablespoons Kraft grated
    parmesan cheese
2 teaspoons Worcestershire sauce
½ teaspoon lemon juice

½ teaspoon ground dry mustard
¼ teaspoon salt
¼ teaspoon garlic powder
¼ teaspoon onion powder
¼ teaspoon ground black pepper
pinch dried basil
pinch dried oregano

Combine all ingredients in a medium bowl and mix with an electric mixer for about 30 seconds. Chill the dressing for a couple hours before serving.

• MAKES 1¼ CUPS.

PACE
PICANTE SAUCE

☆   ♥   ☎   ✎   ✈   ✉   ✂   ☛   ✿

Texan David Pace had been selling 58 different varieties of jam, jellies, and sauces from the back of his liquor store in the 1940s when he came up with a recipe for a thick and spicy tomato-based sauce he dubbed "Picante." When sales of David's new sauce took off, he concentrated all his efforts on marketing his all-natural, preservative-free product, and designed the sauce's famous hourglass-shaped jar (to keep it from tipping over). Now America's number-one Mexican hot sauce brand, Pace Foods makes it known that it still uses only fresh jalapeño peppers in the sauces, rather than the brined, less flavorful jalapeños—like those canned nacho slices. Each year all the fresh jalapeños used by the company weigh in at around 30 million pounds, and the nation gobbles up around 120 million pounds of the zingy sauces. Here's a simple recipe to make a kitchen copy of the medium heat–level Pace Picante Sauce, which was the first variety David created. The mild and hot versions were added in 1981, and you'll find clones for those at the bottom of the recipe in Tidbits.

One 10 ¾-ounce can tomato puree
1 can full of water (1 ⅓ cups)
⅓ cup chopped Spanish onion
¼ cup chopped fresh jalapeño
    peppers, with seeds (3 to 4
    peppers)

2 tablespoons white vinegar
rounded ¼ teaspoon salt
¼ teaspoon dried minced onion
¼ teaspoon dried minced garlic

1. Combine all ingredients in a saucepan over medium high heat.
2. Bring to a boil, reduce heat, and simmer for 30 minutes or until thick.
3. When cool, bottle in 16-ounce jar and refrigerate overnight.

- MAKES 2 CUPS (16 OUNCES).

TIDBITS

For the mild version of the salsa, reduce the amount of fresh jalapeños to 2 rounded tablespoons (2 to 3 peppers).

For the hot variety, increase the amount of jalapeños to ⅓ cup (4 to 5 peppers).

PANDA EXPRESS
MANDARIN CHICKEN

☆   ♥   ☎   ✎   ✈   ✉   ✂   ☛   ✿

Here's a dish from a rapidly growing Chinese food chain that should satisfy anyone who loves the famous marinated bourbon chicken found in food courts across America. The sauce is the whole thing here, and it's quick to make right on your own stove-top. Just fire up the barbecue or indoor grill for the chicken and whip up a little white rice to serve on the side. Panda Express—now 370 restaurants strong—is the fastest-growing Asian food chain in the world. You'll find these tasty little quick-service food outlets in supermarkets, casinos, sports arenas, college campuses, and malls across the country passing out free samples for the asking.

⅔ cup sugar
¼ cup soy sauce
1 tablespoon lemon juice
1 teaspoon vegetable oil
1 teaspoon minced fresh garlic
½ teaspoon minced fresh ginger

¼ cup water
4 teaspoons arrowroot
6 skinless chicken thigh fillets

ON THE SIDE
steamed white rice

1. Combine sugar, soy sauce, lemon juice, oil, garlic, and ginger in a small saucepan. Combine water with arrowroot in a small bowl and stir until arrowroot is dissolved. Add to saucepan and turn heat to high. Stir often while bringing mixture to a boil, then reduce heat and simmer for 4 to 6 minutes or until sauce is thick.
2. Preheat your grill on high for the chicken.

3. When the grill is hot, rub each chicken piece with oil and cook the chicken for 4 to 6 minutes per side or until completely cooked. Chicken should have browned in spots.
4. When chicken is done, chop it into bite-size pieces. Pour the chicken pieces into a large frying pan over medium heat. Heat until chicken sizzles then reduce heat and cover chicken until ready to serve. Spoon chicken into a medium bowl, then pour all the sauce over the chicken and stir until well coated. Serve with steamed white rice.

• SERVES 4.

PANDA EXPRESS
ORANGE FLAVORED CHICKEN

☆　♥　☎　✎　✈　✉　✂　☛　✿

As far as Chinese food goes, I think the stuff these guys throw together in sizzling woks is surprisingly tasty for a takeout chain. This dish is something of a twist on the traditional sweet and sour chicken commonly found at Chinese restaurants over the years. This popular menu item has a delicious, citrus-laced, tangy-sweet sauce with a spicy nip the regulars find truly addictive. The chain claims to cook all of its food in woks, including the sauces. But this homegrown version will work fine—whether you go for a wok, or not.

SAUCE

1½ cups water
2 tablespoons orange juice
1 cup packed dark brown sugar
⅓ cup rice vinegar
2½ tablespoons soy sauce
¼ cup plus 1 teaspoon lemon
　juice
1 teaspoon minced water chestnuts
½ teaspoon minced fresh ginger
¼ teaspoon minced garlic
1 rounded teaspoon chopped
　green onion
¼ teaspoon crushed red pepper
　flakes

5 teaspoons cornstarch
2 teaspoons arrowroot
3 tablespoons water

CHICKEN

4 skinless chicken breast fillets
1 cup ice water
1 egg
¼ teaspoon baking soda
¼ teaspoon salt
1½ cups unsifted cake flour

2 to 4 cups vegetable oil

1. Combine all of the sauce ingredients except the cornstarch, arrowroot, and 3 tablespoons of water in a small saucepan over high heat. Stir often while bringing mixture to a boil. When sauce reaches a boil, remove it from heat and allow it to cool a bit, uncovered.

2. Slice chicken breasts into bite-size chunks. Remove exactly 1 cup of the marinade from the pan and pour it over the chicken in a large resealable plastic bag or another container that allows the chicken to be completely covered with the marinade. The chicken should marinate for at least a couple hours. Cover the remaining sauce and leave it to cool until the chicken is ready.

3. When chicken has marinated, preheat 2 inches of vegetable oil in a wok or skillet to 350 degrees.

4. Combine cornstarch with arrowroot in a small bowl, then add 3 tablespoons of water. Stir until cornstarch and arrowroot have dissolved. Pour this mixture into the sauce and set the pan over high heat. When sauce begins to bubble and thicken, cover and remove it from heat.

5. Beat together the ice water and egg in a medium bowl. Add baking soda and salt.

6. Add ¾ cup of the flour and stir with a fork just until the flour is blended into the mixture. The batter should still be lumpy.

7. Sprinkle another ¼ cup of flour on top of the batter and mix it up with only one or two strokes. Most of the new flour will still be floating on top of the mixture. Put the remaining flour (½ cup) into a separate medium bowl.

8. Dip each piece of chicken first into the flour, then into the batter. Let some of the batter drip off and then slide the chicken into the oil. Fry up to ½ of the chicken pieces at a time for 3 to 4 minutes, or until golden brown. Flip the chicken over halfway through cooking time. Remove the chicken to a rack or paper towels to drain.

9. As the chicken cooks, reheat the sauce left covered on the stove. Stir occasionally.

10. When all of the chicken is done, pour it into a large bowl, and cover with the thickened sauce. Stir gently until all of the pieces are well coated.

• SERVES 4.

PAPA JOHN'S
DIPPING SAUCES

☆ ♥ ☎ 🖉 ✈ ⊠ ✂ ☛ ✿

John Schnatter was only 23 years old when he used 1600 dollars of start-up money to buy a pizza oven and have it installed in the broom closet of an Indiana tavern. John started delivering his hot, fresh pizzas, and in 1984, the first year of his business, he sold 300 to 400 pizzas a week. One year later, he opened the first Papa John's restaurant, and his chain has become another American success story. Today the company has expanded to over 2500 locations in 49 states with revenues of 1.7 billion dollars a year. That makes John's place the country's fastest-growing pizza chain.

John has kept the Papa John's menu simple. You won't find salads or subs or chicken wings on his menu. The company just sells pizza, with side orders of breadsticks and cheesesticks made from the same pizza dough recipe. With each order of breadsticks or cheesesticks comes your choice of dipping sauces. I've got clones here for all three of those tasty sauces. You can use these easy clones as dips for a variety of products, or you can simply make your own breadsticks by baking your favorite pizza dough, then slicing it into sticks. If you want cheesesticks, just brush some of the Garlic Sauce on the dough, then sprinkle it with mozzarella cheese and bake. Slice the baked dough into sticks and use the dipping sauce of your choice. It's a cinch.

SPECIAL GARLIC SAUCE

½ cup margarine   dash salt
¼ teaspoon garlic powder

1. Combine ingredients in a small bowl.
2. Microwave on ½ power for 20 seconds. Stir.

• MAKES ½ CUP.

CHEESE SAUCE

½ cup milk   2 teaspoons juice from canned
2 teaspoons cornstarch   jalapeños (nacho slices)
¼ cup Cheez Whiz

1. Combine cornstarch with milk in a small bowl and stir until cornstarch has dissolved.
2. Add Cheez Whiz and stir to combine. Microwave on high for 1 minute, then stir until smooth.
3. Add juice from jalapeño slices, and stir.

• MAKES ½ CUP.

PIZZA SAUCE

One 10 ¾-ounce can tomato   ¼ teaspoon salt
   puree   ¼ teaspoon oregano
¼ cup water   ⅛ teaspoon basil
1 tablespoon sugar   ⅛ teaspoon thyme
1 teaspoon olive oil   ⅛ teaspoon garlic powder
¼ teaspoon lemon juice

1. Combine ingredients in a small saucepan over medium heat. Bring to a boil.
2. Reduce heat and simmer for 15 to 20 minutes.

• MAKES 1 CUP.

PEPPERIDGE FARM GINGER MAN COOKIES

☆ ♥ ☏ ✎ ✈ ✉ ✂ ☛ ✿

When cloning cookies for the holidays, why not clone the best? Pepperidge Farm's Ginger Man cookies bring a sweet gingery crunch to the seasonal or non-seasonal festivities. And so will your version no matter what shape they end up.

1 cup packed dark brown sugar
¾ cup granulated sugar
½ cup shortening
¼ cup molasses
2 eggs
½ teaspoon vanilla
2 cups all-purpose flour
1 teaspoon baking soda

1 teaspoon baking powder
1 teaspoon ground ginger
1 teaspoon salt
1 teaspoon ground cinnamon
¼ teaspoon ground cloves
red sugar crystals (for cake
    decorating)

1. Preheat oven to 300 degrees.
2. Cream together the sugars, shortening, molasses, eggs, and vanilla in a large bowl. Beat with an electric mixer until smooth.
3. In another large bowl, combine flour, baking soda, baking powder, ginger, salt, cinnamon, and cloves.
4. Add the dry mixture to the wet mixture, stirring while you add it.
5. Roll a portion of the dough out on a heavily floured surface. Roll to under ¼ inch thick. Cut the cookies using a man-shaped cookie cutter, or any other cookie cutter shape you've got in the bottom drawer.

6. Place cookies on an oiled cookie sheet and bake for 15 to 18 minutes. Bake only one cookie sheet of cookies at a time.

- MAKES AROUND 3 DOZEN COOKIES.

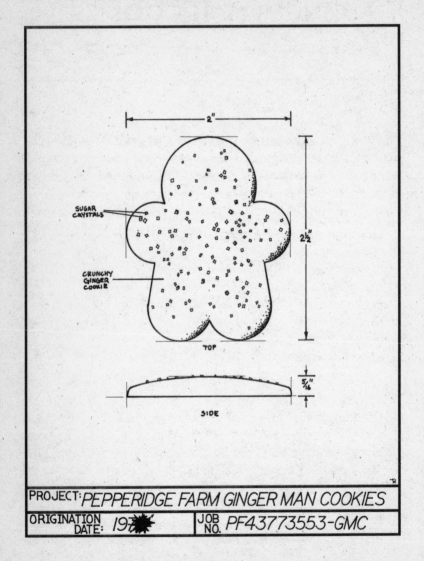

PROGRESSO
ITALIAN-STYLE BREAD CRUMBS

☆　♥　☎　✎　✈　✉　✂　☛　✿

Here's a real easy one that clones the most popular brand of seasoned bread crumbs. Just throw all of the ingredients into a small bowl, mix it up, and you're done. Use the finished product for an Italian-style breading—when frying or baking chicken, fish, pork chops, eggplant, etc.—just as you would the store-bought stuff.

1 cup plain bread crumbs
½ teaspoon salt
½ teaspoon parsley flakes
¼ teaspoon garlic powder

¼ teaspoon onion powder
¼ teaspoon sugar
dash oregano

Combine all ingredients in a small bowl.

• MAKES 1 CUP.

SABRETT
ONIONS IN SAUCE

☆　♥　☎　✎　✈　✉　✄　☛　✿

Here's a cool clone for the tangy orange/red onion sauce slathered over hot dogs ordered from Sabrett's push carts. For a buck or two you can grab a hot dog with the works on the fly from these popular umbrella-covered food carts in many major cities. You find hundreds of 'em in New York City, especially around Central Park. In fact, that's where the sample for this re-creation was obtained. While most of the Sabrett toppings are standard hot dog fare—ketchup, mustard, sauerkraut—the onion sauce is a real Top Secret Recipe. And it's one that we can now slam into the "solved" file.

1 ½ teaspoons olive oil
1 medium onion, sliced thin and chopped
2 cups water
1 tablespoon corn syrup
2 tablespoons tomato paste

1 teaspoon cornstarch
½ teaspoon salt
¼ teaspoon crushed red pepper flakes
¼ cup vinegar

1. Heat the oil in a large saucepan over medium heat.
2. Sauté sliced onion in the oil for 5 minutes, until onions are soft but not brown.
3. Add water, corn syrup, tomato paste, cornstarch, salt, and red pepper flakes, and stir.

4. Bring mixture to a boil, then reduce heat and simmer for 20 minutes. Add vinegar. Continue to simmer for an additional 10 minutes or until most of the liquid has reduced and the sauce is thick.

- MAKES ABOUT 1 ½ CUPS.

SCHILLING
SALAD SUPREME

☆　♥　☎　✎　✈　✉　✂　☛　❀

This orange-colored spice blend has been perking up salads, pasta, potatoes, hamburgers, and vegetables for years now, but I've never seen a homegrown clone for the stuff. Time to change that. While it's obvious that sesame seeds are a major part of this blend, you may not know that the main ingredient is Romano cheese (in the bottle, it's been dyed orange by the paprika). Be sure to store this one in the refrigerator. You might even want to keep the seasoning in an empty shaker-top spice bottle. And if you're in the mood for some tasty pasta salad, just check out the Tidbit below that comes right off the bottle of the original product.

2 tablespoons Romano cheese
1½ teaspoons sesame seeds
1 teaspoon paprika
¾ teaspoon salt
½ teaspoon poppy seeds

½ teaspoon celery seeds
¼ teaspoon garlic powder
¼ teaspoon coarse ground black
　pepper
dash cayenne pepper

1. Combine all ingredients in a small bowl and mix well.
2. Pour blend into a sealed container (such as an empty spice bottle) and store chilled.

- MAKES ¼ CUP.

TIDBITS

The label of the original product includes an easy recipe for Supreme Pasta Salad.

"Combine 1 pound cooked pasta, 8 ounces Italian dressing and 4 tablespoons Salad Supreme [or the amount made in the above clone recipe]. Toss with an assortment of chopped fresh vegetables. Chill."

SUNSHINE
LEMON COOLERS

☆　　♥　　☎　　✎　　✈　　✉　　✂　　☞　　✿

Brothers Jacob and Joseph Loose had a dream of creating products in a bakery filled with sunshine. In 1912 they got their wish by opening the famous "Thousand Window Bakery" in Long Island City, New York. It was the largest bakery in the world until 1955. Today Sunshine Biscuits has moved to another location in Sayerville, New Jersey, where ovens the size of football fields bake like crazy. Sunshine is now owned by Keebler and continues to produce many baked treats you're likely familiar with, such as Hydrox Cookies, Saltine Crackers, Vienna Fingers, Cheez-it Crackers, and these sweet Lemon Coolers. All we have to do is make a few simple adjustments to the Nilla Wafers clone recipe found on page 152, and we can create a cool copy of these awesome little tangy wafer cookies. You know the ones—those little round cookies dusted with lemon-flavored powdered sugar. To make that coating, we'll just use a little unsweetened Kool-Aid lemonade drink mix combined with powdered sugar. Shake the cookies in a bag with this mixture (I call it bake 'n shake) and you've got yourself another tasty knock-off.

½ cup powdered sugar
⅓ cup sugar
⅓ cup shortening
1 egg
½ teaspoon vanilla

⅛ teaspoon salt
1½ cups cake flour
1½ teaspoons baking powder
1 tablespoon water

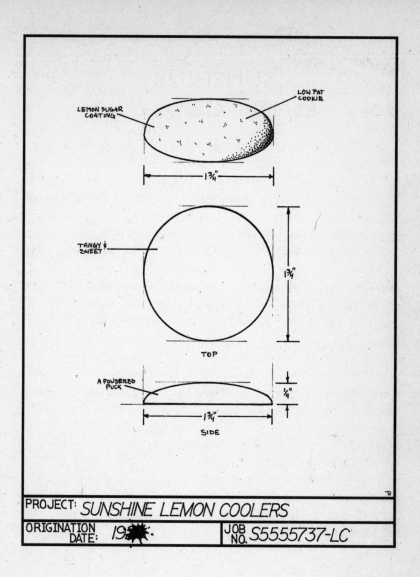

LEMON SUGAR COATING

LOW FAT COOKIE

1¾"

TANGY & SWEET

1¾"

TOP

A POWDERED PUCK

¼"

1¾"

SIDE

PROJECT: *SUNSHINE LEMON COOLERS*

ORIGINATION DATE: 19▮▮

JOB NO. *S5555737-LC*

LEMON POWDERED SUGAR

1 cup powdered sugar

rounded ½ teaspoon Kool-Aid unsweetened lemonade drink mix

1. Preheat oven to 325 degrees.
2. Cream together sugars, shortening, egg, vanilla, and salt in a large bowl.
3. Add the flour and baking powder. Add 1 tablespoon of water and continue mixing until dough forms a ball.
4. Roll dough into ¾-inch balls and flatten slightly onto a lightly greased cookie sheet. Bake for 15 to 18 minutes or until cookies are light brown.
5. As cookies bake, combine 1 cup powdered sugar with the lemonade drink mix in a large plastic bag and shake thoroughly to mix.
6. When the cookies are removed from the oven and while they are hot, add 4 or 5 at a time to the bag and shake it until the cookies are well coated. Repeat with the remaining cookies.

• MAKES 50 TO 56 COOKIES.

TACO BELL
BURRITO SUPREME

☆　♥　☎　✏　✈　✉　✂　☞　✿

To copy Taco Bell's most famous burrito at home you first must assemble the meaty foundation of many of the chain's top-selling products: the spiced ground beef. Toss it and seven other tasty ingredients into a large flour tortilla and fold using the same technique as taught to new recruits at the chain. If you like a bit of heat, throw on some of the hot sauce from the Taco Bell Fire Border Sauce clone recipe found on page 182.

1 pound lean ground beef
1/4 cup all-purpose flour
1 tablespoon chili powder
1 teaspoon salt
1/2 teaspoon dried minced onion
1/2 teaspoon paprika
1/4 teaspoon onion powder
dash garlic powder
1/2 cup water

1 16-ounce can refried beans
8 10-inch flour tortillas
1/2 cup enchilada sauce
3/4 cup sour cream
2 cups shredded lettuce
2 cups shredded cheddar cheese
1 medium tomato, diced
1/2 cup diced yellow onion

1. In a medium bowl, combine the ground beef with the flour, chili powder, salt, minced onion, paprika, onion powder, and garlic powder. Use your hands to thoroughly mix the ingredients into the ground beef.
2. Add the seasoned beef mixture to the water in a skillet over medium heat. Mix well with a wooden spoon or spatula, and

break up the meat as it cooks. Heat for 5 to 6 minutes, or until browned. The finished product should be very smooth, somewhat pasty, with no large chunks of beef remaining.

3. Heat up the refried beans in a covered container in the microwave set on high temperature for 1½ to 2 minutes.

4. Place the flour tortillas in a microwave-safe tortilla steamer, or on a plate and cover with plastic wrap. Heat the tortillas for 30 to 45 seconds in the microwave on high temperature.

5. Build each burrito by first spreading about ¼ cup of refried beans on the center of a heated flour tortilla. Spread one-eighth of the meat mixture over the beans, then pour about a tablespoon of the enchilada sauce over the meat.

6. Stir the sour cream well, so that it is smoother, then spread about 1½ tablespoons onto the burrito. Arrange some of the lettuce, cheese, tomato, and onion onto the tortilla, and then you're ready to roll.

7. Fold the end of the tortilla closest to you over the filling ingredients. Fold either the left or right end over next. Then fold the top edge over the filling. You will be leaving one end of the burrito open and unfolded. Repeat with the remaining ingredients and serve immediately.

• MAKES 8 BURRITOS.

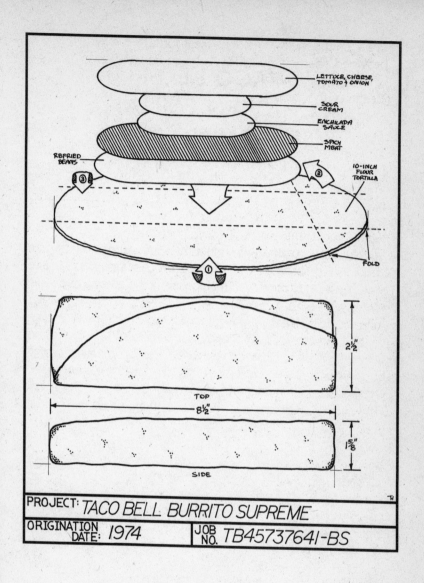

LETTUCE, CHEESE, TOMATO & ONION

SOUR CREAM

ENCHILADA SAUCE

SPICY MEAT

REFRIED BEANS

10-INCH FLOUR TORTILLA

FOLD

②

③

①

2½"

TOP

8½"

1⅝"

SIDE

PROJECT: *TACO BELL BURRITO SUPREME*

ORIGINATION DATE: *1974*

JOB NO. *TB45737641-BS*

TACO BELL CHICKEN FAJITA! SEASONING MIX

☆ ♥ ☏ ✎ ✈ ✉ ✂ ☛ ✿

A couple years ago Taco Bell and Kraft Foods got together to produce a line of products—everything from taco kits to salsas and spice mixes—all stamped with the familiar Taco Bell logo and available in supermarkets across the country. The idea was a winner, and now the Taco Bell line of products is among Kraft's top sellers. The clone of this mix, made with a combination of common spices and cornstarch, can be kept indefinitely until your brain's fajita-craving neurons begin firing. When you're set to cook, you'll just need some chicken, a bell pepper, and an onion, and then you simply follow the same instructions that you find on the package of the real thing, which I've handily included for you below in the recipe.

1 tablespoon cornstarch
2 teaspoons chili powder
1 teaspoon salt
1 teaspoon paprika
1 teaspoon sugar

¾ teaspoon crushed chicken
  bouillon cube
½ teaspoon onion powder
¼ teaspoon garlic powder
¼ teaspoon cayenne pepper
¼ teaspoon cumin

1. Combine all of the ingredients in a small bowl.
2. Prepare fajitas using the following ingredients:

4 skinless chicken breast fillets (1
  to 1¼ pound), cut into thin strips
2 tablespoons oil

⅓ cup water
1 green bell pepper, cut into strips
1 medium onion, sliced

180

Prepare the fajitas using the same directions found on the package of the original seasoning mix:

"1. COOK and stir chicken in hot oil in a large nonstick skillet 5 minutes on medium-high heat. Add TACO BELL Fajita Seasoning Mix, water, green pepper, and onion; cook and stir on medium heat 5 minutes or until chicken is cooked through and the vegetables are tender.
2. PLACE tortillas on microwavable plate. Cover with plastic wrap. Microwave on high 1 minute.
3. SPOON chicken mixture onto each tortilla. Top as desired with TACO BELL salsa. Roll up tortillas."

• MAKES 5 SERVINGS.

TACO BELL
FIRE BORDER SAUCE

☆　♥　☎　✎　✈　⊠　✂　☛　✿

For years Taco Bell customers had only the "mild" and "hot" varieties of free taco sauce blister packs to choose from to add a bit of zing to their fistful of tacos. That is, until the latest addition to the hot sauce selection kicked the heat-o-meter up a few notches. While true hot sauce freaks might find this sauce still on the mild side when compared with the glut of habanero-based sauces on the market today, it's definitely a recipe that improves on the Mexican fast-food chain's original formulas. This one's for those of you who get a rush from a good tastebud tingle.

1 6-ounce can tomato paste	2 teaspoons salt
3 cups water	2 teaspoons cornstarch
3 tablespoons vinegar	1 teaspoon cayenne pepper
3 tablespoons finely minced canned jalapeño slices	1 teaspoon sugar
1 tablespoon chili powder	¼ teaspoon onion powder
1 tablespoon dried minced onion	dash garlic powder

1. Combine the tomato paste with the water in a medium saucepan and whisk until smooth.
2. Add remaining ingredients and stir until combined.
3. Heat mixture over medium high heat until it begins to boil. Continue to cook for about 3 minutes, stirring often. Remove from heat.
4. When sauce has cooled, pour it into a sealed container and refrigerate.

• MAKES 3 CUPS.

TACO BELL
MEXICAN PIZZA

☆　♥　☎　✐　✈　⊠　✂　☞　❀

Hope you're hungry, 'cause this recipe makes four of the Mexican Pizzas like those served at the Bell. Prepare to blow your diners away with this one if they're at all familiar with the real thing.

½ pound ground beef
2 tablespoons all-purpose flour
1½ teaspoons chili powder (Spanish blend is best)
¾ teaspoon salt
¼ teaspoon dried minced onion
¼ teaspoon paprika
dash garlic powder
dash onion powder
2 tablespoons water

1 cup Crisco shortening
8 small (6 inch diameter) flour tortillas
1 16-ounce can refried beans
⅔ cup mild Picante salsa
½ cup shredded cheddar cheese
½ cup shredded Monterey Jack cheese
⅓ cup diced tomato
¼ cup chopped green onion

1. In a medium bowl, combine the ground beef with the flour, chili powder, salt, dried onion, paprika, garlic powder, and onion powder. Use your hands to thoroughly incorporate everything into the ground beef.
2. Preheat a skillet over medium heat and add the ground beef mixture to the pan along with the water. Brown the beef mixture for 5 to 6 minutes, using a wooden spoon or spatula to break up the meat as it cooks.
3. Heat shortening in a frying pan over medium heat. When shortening is hot, fry each tortilla for about 30 to 45 seconds per side and set aside on paper towels. When frying each tor-

tilla, be sure to pop any bubbles that form so that tortilla lies flat in the shortening. Tortillas should become golden brown.

4. Heat up refried beans in a small pan over the stove or in the microwave. Preheat oven to 400 degrees.

5. When meat and tortillas are done, stack each pizza by first spreading about ⅓ cup refried beans on the face of one tortilla. Next spread ¼ to ⅓ cup of meat, then another tortilla. Coat your pizzas with 2 tablespoons of salsa on each, then combine the cheeses and sprinkle the blend evenly over the top of each pizza. Split up the diced tomato and arrange it evenly over the cheese on each pizza, followed by the green onion.

6. Place pizzas in your hot oven for 8 to 12 minutes or until the cheese on top is melted. Cut each pizza into four slices, and serve.

- MAKES 4 PIZZAS.

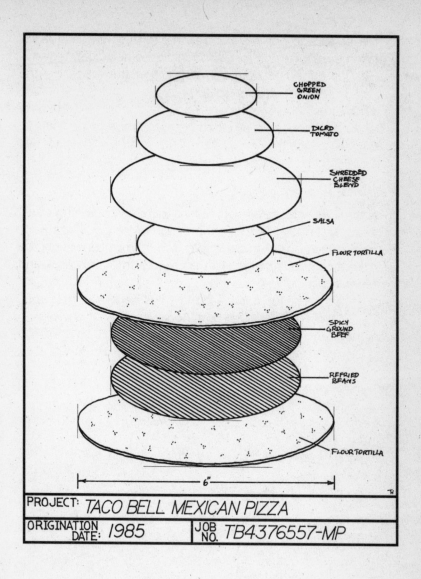

CHOPPED
GREEN
ONION

DICED
TOMATO

SHREDDED
CHEESE
BLEND

SALSA

FLOUR TORTILLA

SPICY
GROUND
BEEF

REFRIED
BEANS

FLOUR TORTILLA

6"

PROJECT: *TACO BELL MEXICAN PIZZA*

ORIGINATION DATE: *1985* JOB NO. *TB4376557-MP*

TACO BELL
SOFT TACO

☆ ♥ ☎ ✎ ✈ ✉ ✄ ☞ ❀

If you don't think those packets of Taco Bell spices you buy in the grocery stores make spiced ground meat that tastes like the stuff they use at the giant Mexican food chain, you'd be correct. If you want the taco meat to taste like the chain's then you're going to have to whip it up from scratch using this original *TSR* recipe. Once you've prepped your meat, the steps below will help you build your tacos the Taco Bell way, hopefully without any pesky talking Chihuahuas running through the kitchen. If you want crispy tacos, just replace the flour tortillas with crunchy corn shells.

1 pound lean ground beef	dash garlic powder
1/4 cup all-purpose flour	1/2 cup water
1 tablespoon chili powder	12 soft taco flour tortillas (6-inch
1 teaspoon salt	tortillas)
1/2 teaspoon dried minced onion	2 cups shredded lettuce
1/2 teaspoon paprika	1 cup shredded cheddar cheese
1/4 teaspoon onion powder	

1. In a medium bowl, combine the ground beef with the flour, chili powder, salt, minced onion, paprika, onion powder, and garlic powder. Use your hands to thoroughly mix the ingredients into the ground beef.
2. Add the seasoned beef mixture to the water in a skillet over medium heat. Mix well with a wooden spoon or spatula, and break up the meat as it cooks. Heat for 5 to 6 minutes, or until browned. The finished product should be very smooth, somewhat pasty, with no large chunks of beef remaining.

3. Heat up the flour tortillas in your microwave for 20 to 30 seconds, or until warm.
4. Build each taco by spooning 2 to 3 tablespoons of the meat into a warm tortilla. Spread some of the shredded lettuce over the meat and then sprinkle some cheese over the top. Repeat with the remaining ingredients and serve immediately.

- MAKES 12 SOFT TACOS.

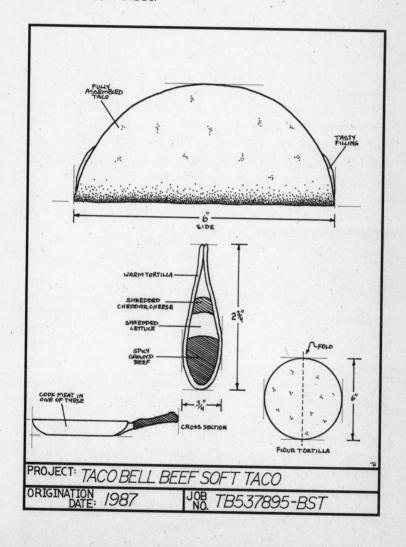

FULLY ASSEMBLED TACO

TASTY FILLING

6"
SIDE

WARM TORTILLA

SHREDDED CHEDDAR CHEESE

SHREDDED LETTUCE

SPICY GROUND BEEF

2 3/4"

FOLD

6"

COOK MEAT IN ONE OF THESE

3/4"

CROSS SECTION

FLOUR TORTILLA

PROJECT: TACO BELL BEEF SOFT TACO

ORIGINATION DATE: 1987

JOB NO. TB537895-BST

TACO BELL
TACO SEASONING MIX

☆　♥　☎　✎　✈　✉　✄　☞　✿

This is a simple recipe to clone the contents of the seasoning packet that bears the Taco Bell logo found in practically all the grocery stores these days. You probably expect the seasoning mix to make meat that tastes exactly like the stuff you get at the big chain. Well, uh, nope. It's more like the popular Lawry's taco seasoning mix, which still makes good spiced ground meat, and works great for a tasty bunch of tacos. But if it's the mushy, spiced meat that's packed into tacos and burritos at America's largest taco joint that you want, you'll have to use the clone recipe for the Taco Bell Soft Taco that precedes this one.

2 tablespoons flour
2 teaspoons chili powder
1½ teaspoons dried minced onion
1¼ teaspoons salt
1 teaspoon paprika
¾ teaspoon crushed beef bouillon
　cube

¼ teaspoon sugar
¼ teaspoon cayenne pepper
¼ teaspoon garlic powder
dash onion powder

1. Combine all of the ingredients in a small bowl.
2. Prepare taco meat using 1 pound of ground beef and following the same spunky directions as on the original package:

   "1. BROWN ground beef; drain. Add seasoning mix and ¾ cup of water. Bring to a boil; reduce heat. Simmer uncovered, 10 minutes, stirring occasionally.
   2. HEAT taco shells or tortillas as directed on package.

3. SERVE bowls of seasoned ground beef, lettuce, tomato, and cheese. Pass the taco shells or tortillas and let everyone PILE ON THE FUN!"

- MAKES 12 TACOS.

TOMMY'S ORIGINAL WORLD FAMOUS HAMBURGERS

☆   ♥   ☎   ✎   ✈   ✉   ✂   ☞   ✿

This clone recipe may be for the whole hamburger, but anybody who knows about Tommy's goes there for the chili—and that's the part of this clone recipe they seek. That's also the part that required the most kitchen sleuthing. Turns out it's an old chili con carne recipe created back in 1946 by Tommy's founder, Tommy Koulax, for his first hamburger stand on the corner of Beverly and Rampart Boulevards in Los Angeles. By adding the right combination of water and flour and broth and spices to the meat we can create a thick, tomato-less chili sauce worthy of the gajillions of southern California college students who make late-night Tommy's runs a four-year habit. And if you don't live near one of the two dozen Tommy's outlets, you can still get a gallon of Tommy's famous chili shipped to you. But I hope you really dig the stuff, because you'll shell out around 70 bucks for the dry ice packaging and overnight shipping. And don't expect to see the ingredients on the label, since the chili comes packed in a gallon-size mustard jug.

CHILI

1 pound ground beef (not lean)
¼ cup flour plus 1¼ cups flour
1⅓ cups beef broth
4 cups water
3 tablespoons chili powder
2 tablespoons grated (and then chopped) carrot

1 tablespoon white vinegar
2 teaspoons dried minced onion
2 teaspoons salt
1 teaspoon granulated sugar
1 teaspoon paprika
¼ teaspoon garlic powder

3 pounds ground beef

8 hamburger buns
16 slices Kraft Singles cheddar
  cheese
½ cup diced onion
32 to 40 hamburger pickles
  (slices)

8 slices large beefsteak tomato
  (½ inch thick)
¼ cup yellow mustard

1. Prepare the chili by first browning the meat in a large sauce-pan over medium heat. Crumble the meat as it browns. When the meat has been entirely cooked (7 to 10 minutes), pour the meat into a strainer over a large cup or saucepan. Let the fat drip out of the meat for about 5 minutes, then return the meat to the first saucepan. Cover and set aside.

2. With the fat from the meat, we will now make a roux—a French contribution to thicker sauces and gravies usually made with fat and flour. Heat the drippings in a saucepan over medium heat (you should have drained off around ½ cup of the stuff). When the fat is hot, add ¼ cup flour to the pan and stir well. Reduce heat to medium low, and continue to heat the roux, stirring often, until it is a rich caramel color. This should take 10 to 15 minutes. Add the beef broth to the pan and stir. Remove from heat.

3. Meanwhile, back at the other pan, add the water to the beef, then whisk in the remaining 1¼ cups flour. Add the roux/broth mixture and the other chili ingredients and whisk until blended. Make sure your grated carrot is chopped up to the size of rice before you add it.

4. Crank the heat up to medium high. Stir often until you see bubbles forming on the surface of the chili. Turn the heat down to medium low, and continue to simmer for 15 to 20 minutes, or until thick. The chili should be calmly bubbling like lava as it simmers. When it's done cooking, take the chili off the heat, cover it, and let it sit for 30 minutes to an hour before using it on the burgers. It should thicken to a tasty brown paste as it sits.

5. To make your hamburgers, you'll first divide 3 pounds of hamburger into 16 portions of 3 ounces each. Grill the burg-

ers in a hot skillet or on an indoor griddle for 4 to 5 minutes per side or until done. Sprinkle some salt and pepper on each patty.

6. Build the burgers by lightly toasting the faces of the hamburger buns. Turn them over into a hot skillet or a griddle on medium heat.
7. Place one patty onto the bottom bun.
8. Position two slices of cheese on the meat.
9. Place another beef patty on the cheese.
10. Spoon about ⅓ cup of chili onto the beef patty.
11. Sprinkle about 1 tablespoon of diced onion onto the chili.
12. Arrange 4 to 5 pickle slices on the onion.
13. Place a thick slice of tomato on next.
14. Spread mustard over the face of the top bun and top off your hamburger by turning this bun over onto the tomato.

• MAKES 8 BURGERS, 6 CUPS OF CHILI.

WENDY'S CHICKEN CAESAR FRESH STUFFED PITA

☆ ♥ ☎ ✎ ✈ ⊠ ✂ ☛ ✿

Early in 1997 Wendy's introduced its selection of cold "Fresh Stuffed" pita sandwiches—perhaps thinking that America was ready for fast food fare that seemed healthier than your standard greasy burger. I love these sandwiches, but apparently most customers didn't agree, since the company discontinued the item in many of the 5000 Wendy's outlets. If you miss the pita sandwiches, and even if you don't, here now is a way to re-create the delicious salads-in-a-flatbread in the comfort of your own home.

DRESSING
1/2 cup water
1/8 teaspoon dry, unflavored gelatin
1/3 cup white vinegar
1/2 cup olive oil
1/2 teaspoon finely minced red bell pepper
1/2 teaspoon salt
1/4 teaspoon garlic powder
1/4 teaspoon Worcestershire sauce
1/8 teaspoon coarse ground black pepper
dash parsley
dash oregano
dash thyme
dash basil

1 tablespoon grated Romano cheese
1 tablespoon grated Parmesan cheese
2 tablespoons egg substitute

2 skinless chicken breast fillets
salt
pepper
6 cups romaine lettuce, chopped
1/4 cup red cabbage, shredded
1/4 cup carrot, shredded
4 pita breads (pocketless, if you can find them)
4 teaspoons shredded, fresh Parmesan cheese

1. Make the dressing by first dissolving the gelatin in the water. Heat the mixture in the microwave on high for 2 minutes or until it begins to boil rapidly. Add the vinegar, then whisk while adding the oil. Add bell pepper, salt, garlic powder, Worcestershire, black pepper, parsley, oregano, thyme, and basil. Let dressing cool for about 15 minutes before adding cheeses and egg substitute. Whisk until slightly thicker, then chill. Overnight refrigeration makes the dressing thicker.
2. Preheat a barbecue or indoor grill to medium heat. Salt and pepper the chicken, then grill it for 5 minutes per side, or until done. Remove chicken from the grill and dice it.
3. While chicken cooks, prepare the salad by combining the romaine lettuce, red cabbage, and shredded carrot in a large bowl and toss.
4. Prepare the sandwiches by first microwaving each pita for 20 seconds.
5. Fold each pita in half like a taco, then add 1 to 1½ cups of the romaine salad into the bread.
6. Add about ⅓ cup of diced chicken on top of the salad in the pita.
7. Pour about a tablespoon of dressing over each sandwich.
8. Sprinkle about a teaspoon of shredded fresh Parmesan on top of each one and serve.

• SERVES 4.

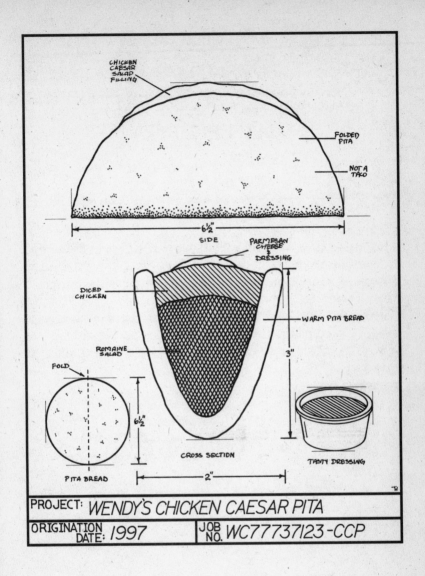

CHICKEN CAESAR SALAD FILLING

FOLDED PITA

NOT A TACO

6½"

SIDE

PARMESAN CHEESE & DRESSING

DICED CHICKEN

WARM PITA BREAD

ROMAINE SALAD

3"

FOLD

6½"

CROSS SECTION

PITA BREAD

2"

TASTY DRESSING

PROJECT: WENDY'S CHICKEN CAESAR PITA

ORIGINATION DATE: 1997

JOB NO. WC77737123-CCP

WENDY'S CLASSIC GREEK FRESH STUFFED PITA

☆　♥　☎　✎　✈　✉　✂　☞　✿

The Classic Greek Pita uses the same salad base and dressing as the previous clone for the Chicken Caesar Pita, but replaces the chicken and Parmesan with a Greek topping that's a breeze to make. Even though Wendy's uses a special custom pocketless pita that can be tough to find in stores, you can use the more common pocketed pita, just without opening the pocket. Instead, you heat up the pita, then fill up the center and fold it like a soft taco.

DRESSING

½ cup water
⅛ teaspoon dry, unflavored gelatin
⅓ cup white vinegar
½ cup olive oil
½ teaspoon finely minced red bell pepper
½ teaspoon salt
¼ teaspoon garlic powder
¼ teaspoon Worcestershire sauce
⅛ teaspoon coarse ground black pepper
dash parsley
dash oregano
dash thyme
dash basil

1 tablespoon grated Romano cheese
1 tablespoon grated Parmesan cheese
2 tablespoons egg substitute

1 cup (4-ounce package) crumbled feta cheese
½ cup tomato, seeded and diced
¼ cup cucumber, thinly sliced and chopped
¼ cup red onion, diced
6 cups romaine lettuce, chopped
¼ cup red cabbage, shredded
¼ cup carrot, shredded
4 pita breads (pocketless, if you can find them)

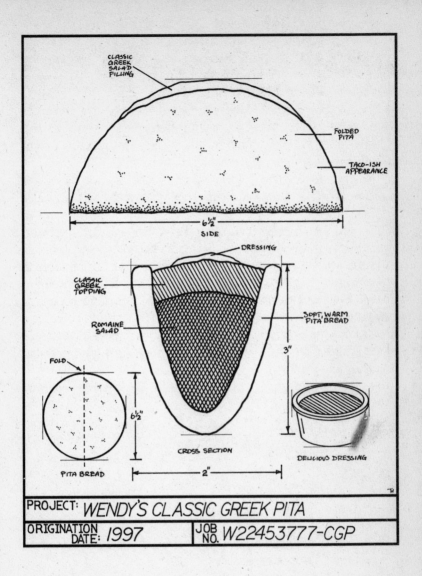

CLASSIC
GREEK
SALAD
FILLING

FOLDED
PITA

TACO-ISH
APPEARANCE

6½"

SIDE

DRESSING

CLASSIC
GREEK
TOPPING

ROMAINE
SALAD

SOFT, WARM
PITA BREAD

3"

FOLD

6½"

CROSS SECTION

PITA BREAD

2"

DELICIOUS DRESSING

PROJECT: *WENDY'S CLASSIC GREEK PITA*

ORIGINATION
DATE: *1997*

JOB
NO. *W22453777-CGP*

1. Make the dressing by first dissolving the gelatin in the water. Heat the mixture in the microwave on high for 2 minutes or until it begins to boil rapidly. Add the vinegar, then whisk while adding the oil. Add bell pepper, salt, garlic powder, Worcestershire, black pepper, parsley, oregano, thyme, and basil. Let dressing cool for about 15 minutes before adding cheeses and egg substitute. Whisk until slightly thicker, then chill. Overnight refrigeration makes the dressing thicker.
2. Make the Greek topping for the sandwiches by combining the crumbled feta cheese, tomato, cucumber, and red onion in a small bowl.
3. Prepare the salad by combining the romaine lettuce, red cabbage, and shredded carrot in a large bowl and toss.
4. Prepare the sandwiches by first microwaving each pita for 20 seconds.
5. Fold each pita in half like a taco, then add 1 to 1½ cups of the romaine salad into the bread.
6. Add ½ to ⅓ cup of the Greek topping to each sandwich.
7. Pour about a tablespoon of dressing over each sandwich and serve.

- SERVES 4.

WENDY'S
SPICY CHICKEN FILLET
SANDWICH

☆　♥　☎　✎　✈　✉　✂　☞　✿

There once was a time when Wendy's offered this sandwich for a "limited time only." Apparently the tasty zing from this breaded chicken sandwich won it many loyal customers and a permanent place on the fast food chain's menu. Now you can re-create the spicy kick of the original with a secret blend of spices in the chicken's crispy coating. Follow the same stacking order as the original, and you've just made four sandwich clones at a fraction of the cost of the real thing.

6 to 8 cups vegetable oil
1/3 cup Frank's Original Red Hot Pepper Sauce
2/3 cup water
1 cup all-purpose flour
2 1/2 teaspoons salt
4 teaspoons cayenne pepper
1 teaspoon coarse ground black pepper

1 teaspoon onion powder
1/2 teaspoon paprika
1/8 teaspoon garlic powder
4 skinless chicken breast fillets
4 plain hamburger buns
8 teaspoons mayonnaise
4 lettuce leaves
4 tomato slices

1. Preheat 6 to 8 cups of oil in a deep fryer to 350 degrees.
2. Combine the pepper sauce and water in a small bowl.
3. Combine the flour, salt, cayenne pepper, black pepper, onion powder, paprika, and garlic powder in another shallow bowl.
4. Pound each of the chicken pieces with a mallet until about

⅜-inch thick. Trim each breast fillet if necessary to help it fit on the bun.

5. Working with one fillet at a time, coat each piece with the flour, then dredge it in the diluted pepper sauce. Coat the chicken once again in the flour mixture and set it aside until the rest of the chicken is coated.

6. Fry the chicken fillets for 8 to 12 minutes or until they are light brown and crispy. Remove the chicken to a rack or to paper towels to drain.

7. As chicken is frying, prepare each sandwich by grilling the face of the hamburger buns on a hot skillet over medium heat. Spread about 2 teaspoons of mayonnaise on the face of each of the inverted top buns.

8. Place a tomato slice onto the mayonnaise, then stack a leaf of lettuce on top of the tomato.

9. On each of the bottom buns, stack one piece of chicken.

10. Flip the top half of each sandwich onto the bottom half and serve hot.

• MAKES 4 SANDWICHES.

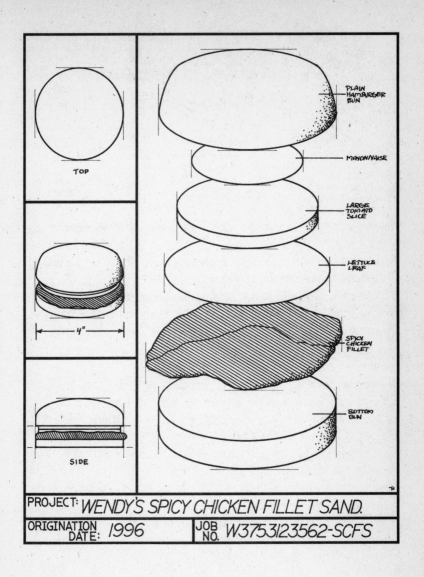

TOP

4"

SIDE

PLAIN
HAMBURGER
BUN

MAYONNAISE

LARGE
TOMATO
SLICE

LETTUCE
LEAF

SPICY
CHICKEN
FILLET

BOTTOM
BUN

PROJECT: *WENDY'S SPICY CHICKEN FILLET SAND.*

ORIGINATION DATE: *1996*

JOB NO. *W3753123562-SCFS*

WIENERSCHNITZEL CHILI SAUCE

☆　♥　☎　✎　✈　⊠　✄　☞　✿

The real version of this chili sauce comes to each Wienerschnitzel unit in big 'ol 6-pound, 12-ounce cans of concentrated brown goo with bits of ground pork already in it. But after adding 64 ounces of water and 15 chopped hamburger patties to the sauce the magic begins to happen; the stuff transforms into the familiar thick and spicy chili sauce that gets dolloped over hot dogs and french fries for the drooling customers at America's largest hot dog chain. The proper proportion of spices, tomato paste, and meat is crucial, but the real challenge in cloning this recipe is figuring out a common grocery store equivalent for the "modified food starch" that's used in large quantities in the real chili sauce as a thickener. After a couple days sealed up in the underground lab with Starbucks lattes on intravenous drip, I finally came out squinting at the bright sunshine—victorious—with a killer solution to the chili conundrum! This secret combination of cornstarch and Wondra flour (and plenty of salt and chili powder) gives you a chili sauce that says nothing but "Wienerschnitzel" all over it (even without the MSG!). So get out the hot dogs, baby! The top requested secret clone recipe from this 40-year-old chain has finally been cracked.

¾ pound ground beef
¼ pound ground pork
6 cups water
¼ cup cornstarch

½ cup Wondra flour (see Tidbits)
6-ounce can tomato paste
¼ cup chili powder (McCormick)
3 tablespoons white vinegar

1 tablespoon salt	¼ teaspoon garlic powder
1 tablespoon dried minced onion	¼ teaspoon ground black pepper
1½ teaspoons granulated sugar	

1. Brown ground beef and ground pork in a large saucepan over medium heat. Crumble and chop the meat with a spoon or spatula as it cooks. When the meat is completely browned cover saucepan and turn heat to low. This way the ground meat will slowly simmer in its own juices.
2. After 10 minutes, remove the ground meat from the heat and drain off most of the fat. Keep some of it in the pan.
3. While the meat is still off the heat add the water and the cornstarch to the pan. Whisk the cornstarch thoroughly as it's added until it's dissolved into the water. Do the same for the Wondra flour.
4. You can now set the pan back over medium heat and add the remaining ingredients. Bring mixture to a boil, stirring often.
5. When chili begins to boil, reduce heat and simmer for 30 minutes. When chili is done it will be much thicker and darker, like the real thing. And, like the original, you can use this chili sauce on hot dogs, hamburgers, and french fries, or take it solo.

- MAKES 6 CUPS.

TIDBITS

Wondra flour is a finely ground, quick-mixing flour used in sauces and gravies. It is made by Gold Medal and can usually be found in the baking aisle next to all the other flours.

TRADEMARKS

Arby's and Bronco Berry Sauce are registered trademarks of Arby's, Inc.

Auntie Anne's is a registered trademark of Auntie Anne's, Inc.

Baskin-Robbins is a registered trademark of Baskin-Robbins, Inc.

Boston Market, McDonald's, Arch Deluxe, BigXtra!, Breakfast Bagel Sandwiches, Breakfast Burrito, and Big Mac are registered trademarks of McDonald's Corporation

Bull's-Eye, Good Seasons, Kraft, Shake 'n Bake, Stove Top, Nabisco, Cheese Nips, and Nilla are registered trademarks of Kraft Foods, Inc.

Burger King, BK Broiler, Big King, and Croissan'wich are registered trademarks of Burger King Corporation.

Cadbury's is a registered trademark of Cadbury USA, Inc.

Carl's Jr. is a registered trademark of Carl Karcher Enterprises, Inc.

Chef Paul Prudhomme's and Poultry Magic are registered trademarks of Magic Seasoning Blends, Inc.

Cinnabon and CinnabonStix are registered trademarks of AFC Enterprises

Dolly Madison, Zingers, Drake's, and Devil Dogs are registered trademarks of Interstate Brands Bakeries Corporation

DoubleTree is a registered trademark of Hilton Hospitality, Inc.

Emeril's is a registered trademark of Emeril's Food of Love Productions

Fatburger is a registered trademark of Fatburger Corporation

French's and Classic Yellow are registered trademarks of Reckitt Benckiser, Inc.

Girl Scout and Thin Mints are registered trademarks of Girl Scouts USA

GrandMa's is a registered trademark of Frito-Lay, Inc.

Great American Cookies is a registered trademark of Mrs. Fields Brands, Inc.

Heinz and Heinz 57 are registered trademarks of H.J. Heinz Co.

Hershey's and PayDay are registered trademarks of Hershey Foods Corporation

HoneyBaked is a registered trademark of the HoneyBaked Ham Company

Hot Dog on a Stick is a registered trademark of HDOS Enterprises

K.C. Masterpiece is a registered trademark of The Clorox Company

Kellogg's and Rice Krispies Treats are registered trademarks of Kellogg Company

Kenny Rogers Roasters is a registered trademark of Nathan's Famous, Inc.

KFC, Extra Crispy, Honey BBQ Wings, Taco Bell, Burrito Supreme, and Fire Border Sauce are registered trademarks of Tricon Global Restaurants, Inc.

Lawry's is a registered trademark of Lawry's, Inc.

Little Debbie is a registered trademark of McKee Foods Corporation

Mrs. Dash is a registered trademark of Alberto-Culver USA, Inc.

Nestlé and Baby Ruth are registered trademarks of Nestlé S.A.

Newman's Own is a registered trademark of Newman's Own, Inc.

Pace and Pepperidge Farm are registered trademarks of Campbell's Soup Company

Panda Express is a registered trademark of Panda Management Company, Inc.

Papa John's is a registered trademark of Papa John's International, Inc.

Progresso is a registered trademark of Progresso Quality Foods Company

Sabrett is a registered trademark of Marathon Enterprises, Inc.

Schilling and Salad Supreme are registered trademarks of McCormick & Co., Inc.

Sunshine and Lemon Coolers are registered trademarks of Keebler Company

Original Tommy's is a trademark of Original Tommy's, Inc.

Wendy's and Fresh Stuffed Pita are registered trademarks of Wendy's International

Wienerschnitzel is a registered trademark of Galardi Group, Inc.

INDEX

More Top Secret Recipes from
TODD WILBUR

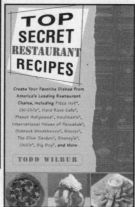

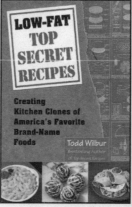

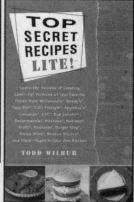